W9-AEU-043

Russia's Wrong Direction: What the United States Can and Should Do

Russia's Wrong Direction: What the United States Can and Should Do

Report of an Independent Task Force

Sponsored by the Council on Foreign Relations

Founded in 1921, the Council on Foreign Relations is an independent, national membership organization and a nonpartisan center for scholars dedicated to producing and disseminating ideas so that individual and corporate members, as well as policymakers, journalists, students, and interested citizens in the United States and other countries, can better understand the world and the foreign policy choices facing the United States and other governments. The Council does this by convening meetings; conducting a wide-ranging Studies program; publishing *Foreign Affairs*, the preeminent journal covering international affairs and U.S. foreign policy; maintaining a diverse membership; sponsoring Independent Task Forces; and providing up-to-date information about the world and U.S. foreign policy on the Council's website, www.cfr.org.

THE COUNCIL TAKES NO INSTITUTIONAL POSITION ON POLICY ISSUES AND HAS NO AFFILIATION WITH THE U.S. GOVERNMENT. ALL STATEMENTS OF FACT AND EXPRESSIONS OF OPINION CONTAINED IN ITS PUBLICA-TIONS ARE THE SOLE RESPONSIBILITY OF THE AUTHOR OR AUTHORS.

The Council will sponsor an Independent Task Force when (1) an issue of current and critical importance to U.S. foreign policy arises, and (2) it seems that a group diverse in backgrounds and perspectives may, nonetheless, be able to reach a meaningful consensus on a policy through private and nonpartisan deliberations. Typically, a Task Force meets between two and five times over a brief period to ensure the relevance of its work.

Upon reaching a conclusion, a Task Force issues a report, and the Council publishes its text and posts it on the Council website. Task Force reports reflect a strong and meaningful policy consensus, with Task Force members endorsing the general policy thrust and judgments reached by the group, though not necessarily every finding and recommendation. Task Force members who join the consensus may submit additional or dissenting views, which are included in the final report. "Chairman's Reports" are signed by Task Force chairs only and are usually preceded or followed by full Task Force reports. Upon reaching a conclusion, a Task Force may also ask individuals who were not members of the Task Force to associate themselves with the Task Force report to enhance its impact. All Task Force reports "benchmark" their findings against current administration policy in order to make explicit areas of agreement and disagreement. The Task Force is solely responsible for its report. The Council takes no institutional position.

For further information about the Council or this Task Force, please write to the Council on Foreign Relations, 58 East 68th Street, New York, NY 10021, or call the Communications office at 212-434-9400. Visit our website at www.cfr.org.

Copyright © 2006 by the Council on Foreign Relations®, Inc.
All rights reserved.
Printed in the United States of America.

This report may not be reproduced in whole or in part, in any form beyond the reproduction permitted by Sections 107 and 108 of the U.S. Copyright Law Act (17 U.S.C. Sections 107 and 108) and excerpts by reviewers for the public press, without express written permission from the Council on Foreign Relations. For information, write to the Publications Office, Council on Foreign Relations, 58 East 68th Street, New York, NY 10021.

Task Force Chairs

John Edwards

John Edwards

Jack Kemp

Jack Kemp

Project Director

Stephen Sestanovich

Stephen Sestanovich

Task Force Members

Stephen E. Biegun

Coit D. Blacker

Robert D. Blackwill*

Antonina W. Bouis

Mark F. Brzezinski

Richard R. Burt*

John Edwards

Robert J. Einhorn

John Lewis Gaddis

John A. Gordon

James A. Harmon

Steven E. Hellman

Fiona Hill

Jack Kemp

Clifford A. Kupchan

Jessica T. Mathews

Michael A. McFaul

Mark C. Medish

Stephen Sestanovich

David R. Slade*

Walter B. Slocombe*

Strobe Talbott

Judyth L. Twigg

Margaret D. Williams

Dov S. Zakheim*

*The individual has endorsed the report and submitted an additional or a dissenting view.

Contents

Foreword

The United States has generally enjoyed good relations with Russia since the dissolution of the Soviet Union fifteen years ago. Washington, Moscow, and the world have benefited from this cooperation on issues ranging from weapons proliferation to counterterrorism after the terrorist attacks of September 11, 2001.

In recent years, however, particularly during the second term of Russian President Vladimir Putin, Russian society and foreign policy have continued to change in ways that raise questions and cause problems for the United States. The Council on Foreign Relations established an Independent Task Force in the spring of 2005 to take stock of developments in Russia, assess the U.S.-Russian relationship, and offer a broad strategy and a set of recommendations for U.S. policymakers in light of these developments.

The Task Force's opening premise is that sustaining cooperation with Russia remains important to the United States. On a number of issues—Iran, energy, HIV/AIDS, and preventing terrorists from acquiring weapons of mass destruction—Russia's cooperation is seen as central to promoting American interests. The Task Force finds, however, that in many areas, U.S.-Russian relations are a disappointment. The Task Force recommends that the United States pursue "selective cooperation" with Russia rather than seek a broad "partnership" that is not now feasible.

In reviewing domestic developments in Russia, the Task Force concludes that Russia is "headed in the wrong direction" despite impressive economic development and the growth of the middle class. The Task Force argues that domestic developments in Russia are of consequence to the United States for strategic as well as moral reasons, and that U.S. policymakers should address themselves both to what happens inside Russia as well as to more traditional U.S. foreign policy concerns.

The Council is indebted to John Edwards and Jack Kemp for serving as chairs of this important group. They devoted ten months of intensive effort to this project, including an important trip to Moscow in the fall of 2005, where they met with senior government officials, business leaders, scholars, and democracy activists. They not only drove this group toward a strong consensus but also helped to bring international attention to the efforts of the Duma (the lower house of Russia's parliament) to intimidate or put out of business foreign and Russian nongovernmental organizations. The Task Force also comprised many of America's preeminent Russia scholars and policy practitioners. The membership constitutes a broad and diverse range of experience. Working with the chairs, the Task Force members have produced a report that bears an important message, one that I expect will reverberate in the United States, Russia, and beyond. Finally, I wish to thank Ambassador Stephen Sestanovich, the Council's George F. Kennan senior fellow for Russian and Eurasian studies, who has written a thoughtful and challenging report.

Richard N. Haass
President
Council on Foreign Relations
March 2006

Acknowledgments

The Independent Task Force on U.S. policy toward Russia, sponsored by the Council on Foreign Relations, has benefited throughout its deliberations from the leadership of Jack Kemp and John Edwards. A group like ours needs many things from its chairs, none of which are more important than the reality checks that only two national political figures can provide. It has been a real pleasure to work with them.

Though independence is in our name, the Task Force is eager to acknowledge the contributions of those on whom it has depended most since meeting for the first time in May 2005. Lee Feinstein, director of the Council's Task Force program, enabled the group to understand what Task Forces are supposed to do, and then to do it; an old Russia hand himself, he sharpened our thinking at every stage. Other Council colleagues were also a huge help. Rositsa J. Petrova and Lindsay Workman carried the burden of research and organization with energy and skill. Lisa Shields, Anya Schmemann, and Irina Faskianos oversaw an ambitious outreach effort. Patricia Dorff and Molly Graham put the manuscript into its final form on very short notice, and even made it look nice.

Derek H. Chollet, as an adviser to Senator Edwards, and James R. "J.T." Taylor, as managing partner of Kemp Partners, made it possible for three organizations to work together smoothly—and enjoy it. Bona Park and Kathleen McGlynn solved all our scheduling problems.

Special thanks go to Steven E. Hellman, Judyth L. Twigg, Fiona Hill, Mark F. Brzezinski, Walter B. Slocombe, Robert E. Einhorn, and Michael A. McFaul for briefing the rest of the Task Force at our early meetings. Mark C. Medish, Stephen E. Biegun, and Walter B. Slocombe chaired subgroups on crime and corruption, trade, and nuclear policy, respectively. Jessica T. Mathews helped us understand the significance of last fall's draft legislation on Russian nongovernmental organizations. Elizabeth Sherwood-Randall, with encouragement from George Joulwan, prepared a highly informative memo on military cooperation before the chairs' trip to Moscow. Judyth Twigg and Margaret D. Williams get the credit for the report's user-friendly text boxes on demographic and environmental issues. But these are special thanks only—the vigor and value of our discussions were sustained by all members of the group, who then lavished much red ink on the draft manuscript.

The Task Force is grateful to the distinguished scholars and specialists to whom we turned many times for ideas and advice. For their help, our thanks to Daniel H. Yergin of Cambridge Energy Research Associates; Robert Legvold of Columbia University; Matthew Bunn of Harvard University; David G. Victor of Stanford University; Jeremy R. Azrael of the Rand Corporation; Z. Blake Marshall of the U.S.-Russia Business Council; Andrew C. Kuchins, Rose E. Gottemoeller, Dmitri Trenin, Lilia Shevtsova, and Masha Lipman of the Carnegie Moscow Center; and Denis A. Maslov of the Eurasia Group.

Many who helped the group by meeting with its members—particularly with the chairs during their fact-finding trip to Moscow—will probably be happiest receiving our thanks anonymously. Suffice it to say that these meetings included senior Russian and American diplomats; Kremlin and White House officials; Russian and American parliamentarians; Russian, American, and European business leaders; Russian, American, and European journalists; and Russian and American policy analysts, political activists, and chess players. Richard G. Lugar and Sam Nunn were generous in sharing their unique impressions from their recent visits to Russia.

The Task Force is particularly grateful to Richard N. Haass, president of the Council on Foreign Relations, for seeing that the state of U.S.-Russian relations called for a policy review and for preserving the group's independence where it matters most—in the substance of our report.

Finally, the Council on Foreign Relations expresses its thanks to David M. Rubenstein for his generous support of the Task Force program.

Stephen Sestanovich
Project Director

Map

Source: From http://www.cia.gov/cia/publications/factbook/maps/rs–map.gif.

Task Force Report

Introduction and Overview

Fifteen years after the end of the Cold War, it is time to take stock of what has, and has not, been accomplished in the effort to create a "strategic partnership" between Russia and the United States. Russia is not the same country it was a decade and a half ago. It is not even the same country it was when President Vladimir Putin took office in May 2000. U.S.-Russian relations have changed as well.

Since the dissolution of the Soviet Union, American presidents and policymakers have believed that the interests of the United States are served by engagement with Russia. This Task Force, too, began its review of U.S. policy—and concludes it—convinced of the extraordinary importance of getting U.S. relations with Russia right.

U.S.-Russian cooperation can help the United States to handle some of the most difficult challenges it faces: terrorism, the proliferation of weapons of mass destruction, tight energy markets, climate change, the drug trade, infectious diseases, and human trafficking. These problems are more manageable when the United States has Russia on its side rather than aligned against it.

Good relations between Moscow and Washington also bolster one of the most promising international realities of our time—the near absence of security rivalries among the major powers. That the world's leading states deal with each other in a spirit of accommodation is a great asset for American policy, and the United States will be in a better position to protect that arrangement if relations with Russia are on a positive track.

Today's U.S.-Russian relationship can be credited with real achievements:

- Cooperative programs to increase the physical security of nuclear materials and sensitive technologies help to keep them out of dangerous hands.

- Growing trade and investment benefit Americans and contribute to Russia's social and economic modernization.

- Russian and American policymakers are—at least for now—working together to reduce the risk that Iran will acquire nuclear weapons. Containing Tehran's nuclear aspirations depends in large part on how closely and effectively Moscow and Washington collaborate.

Yet U.S.-Russian relations are now also marked by a growing number of disagreements. Cooperation is becoming the exception, not the norm, and what leaders of both countries have called a "partnership" is not living up to its potential.

- At a time when the president of the United States has made democracy a goal of American foreign policy, Russia's political system is becoming steadily more authoritarian. Russia is a less open and less democratic society than it was just a few years ago, and the rollback of political pluralism and centralization of power there may not have run their course.

- Russia has used energy exports as a policy weapon—intervening in Ukraine's politics, putting pressure on its foreign policy choices, and curtailing supplies to the rest of Europe. The reassertion of government control over the Russian energy sector increases the risk that this weapon will be used again.

- Russia and the United States may also be starting to diverge in their responses to the threat of terrorism. Russia has tried to curtail U.S. access to bases in Central Asia that support military operations in Afghanistan. President Putin raised further questions when, after agreeing with the United States and the European Union (EU) not to have high-level contact with Hamas, he invited its leaders to Moscow.

- Russia's policies toward the states on its periphery have become a recurrent source of friction between Moscow and Washington and are increasingly entwined with other issues, including energy, counterterrorism, and support for democratic reform.

With disagreements of this kind on the rise, U.S.-Russian relations are clearly headed in the wrong direction. Contention is crowding out consensus. The very idea of "strategic partnership" no longer seems realistic.

How should America deal with this downward trajectory? Some have suggested a narrower focus: choose one or two interests—nonproliferation, for example—and keep disagreement over Russia's growing authoritarianism from undermining cooperation on these priorities. Others favor a process of disengagement: exclude Russia from forums, especially those of the Group of Eight (G8), that are supposed to reflect common values.

We do not believe that either of these approaches is correct. In America's relations with Russia, the choice between interests and values is a false one. It misreads the connection between internal developments in Russia and the broader foreign policy interests of the United States.

- On an issue such as the proliferation of nuclear weapons, both sides are guided by calculations of national security. They will not cease to cooperate merely because they disagree on other matters.

- Moreover, disagreements between Moscow and Washington are not confined to the realm of "values." Russian and American approaches to major issues such as energy security and counterterrorism are also diverging. The gap between them will not be closed merely because the United States is less critical of Russian authoritarianism.

Above all, concern about Russia's domestic evolution should not be seen as a matter of values alone.

- It reflects growing doubt about whether Russia is building a modern and effective state that can cooperate successfully with other modern nations to deal with common problems.

- Despite rapid economic growth and social transformation, Russian political institutions are becoming neither more modern nor more effective, but corrupt and brittle. As a result, Russia's capacity to address security concerns of fundamental importance to the United States and its allies is reduced. And many kinds of cooperation—from securing nuclear materials to intelligence sharing—are undermined.

- Today, Russia seems stable, but its stability has a weak institutional base. The future of its political system is less predictable—and the country's problems are less manageable—than they should be.

The list of issues that matter in U.S.-Russian relations is too long and too important to be shortened to one or two overriding security concerns. We believe that current American policy is right to have a broad agenda, but that the United States needs a more effective strategy to achieve its goals.

- To create a stronger foundation for working together on securing nuclear materials in Russia and to promote a common strategy on Iran, the United States should deepen its cooperation with Russia on a range of other nuclear issues as well. Moscow and Washington should negotiate an agreement that will for the first time create the legal basis for working together on civilian nuclear energy projects, including international spent-fuel storage.

- To limit Russia's use of oil and gas exports as an instrument of coercion—and as a prop for authoritarianism—the United States needs to agree with other governments, especially those of its European allies, on measures to assure that state-controlled Russian energy companies act like true commercial entities. Such an effort cannot succeed in a vacuum; it underscores the vital importance of developing a comprehensive energy policy.

- To ease Russian pressure on neighboring states, the United States should work to accelerate those states' integration into the West. Post-Soviet states that share America's approach to major international problems and can contribute to resolving them should be able to count on greater support.

- To go beyond mere expressions of concern about the rollback of Russian democracy, the United States should increase, not cut, funding under the Freedom Support Act, focusing in particular on organizations committed to free and fair parliamentary and presidential elections in 2007–2008. Russia's course will not—and must not—be set by foreigners, but the United States and its allies cannot be indifferent to the legitimacy of this process and to the leaders it produces. Working with Congress, American policymakers need to elaborate—publicly and privately—the criteria that they will employ in judging the conduct of these elections.

- To protect the credibility of the G8 at a time when many are questioning Russia's chairmanship of that group, the United States should make clear that this role does not exempt Russian policies and actions from critical scrutiny. Keeping the G8 a viable international forum will require a de facto revival of the Group of Seven (G7). Without creating a completely new forum, the United States and its democratic allies have to assume a stronger coordinating role within the existing one.

Current U.S. policy toward Russia tries to capitalize on areas of agreement, while muting issues of discord. Our approach is different: We favor doing more to build on existing agreement, but more as well to advance American interests in areas where Russian and U.S. policies are at odds. This approach will help to get the most out of the relationship in the short run, while encouraging its transformation in the long run.

Urging Russia to take a more democratic direction must be done with great care. America will not succeed if it is seen to be hypercritical, hypocritical, or excessively meddlesome. It will be easy to alienate a Russian public, already prone to xenophobia, that knows of Washington's close relations with many states whose societies are not nearly as open as Russia's. The United States and its allies should not belittle Russia by subjecting it to double standards but should show respect by holding Russia to high ones. By speaking in unison, the United States and its allies can make clear that their goal is not to prevail in a post–Cold War test of strength, but to draw Russia back into the Western mainstream.

Over time, accumulating disagreements between Russia and the United States can have consequences that go well beyond a downturn in bilateral relations. They raise the prospect of a broader weakening of unity among the leading states of the international system. If growing consensus among the major powers gives way to a new line of division between democrats and authoritarians, if their energy strategies diverge, or if they respond in different ways to terrorism, America's chances of success in meeting global challenges will be reduced. At present, the risk that such divisions will emerge may seem remote, but policymakers should not fail to anticipate the tipping point. And Americans should understand how much Russia's future course—above all, whether its policies look West or East—can affect the outcome.

Since the end of the Cold War, successive American administrations have sought to create a relationship with Russia that they called "partnership." This is the right long-term goal, but it is unfortunately not a realistic prospect for U.S.-Russian relations over the next several years. The real question that the United States faces in this period is not how to make partnership with Russia work, it is how to make selective cooperation—and in some cases selective opposition—serve important international goals.

To understand how American options have narrowed in this way, we have to turn to the achievements and disappointments of U.S.-Russian relations in recent years and, even more, to the dramatic changes that are remaking Russia itself. Those changes will determine whether real partnership becomes more attainable in the future than it is now.

Russia's Social and Economic Transformation . . .

The watchword of the Putin era is stability, but its true distinguishing feature is change—political, economic, and social. The changes underway, moreover, point in very different directions and imply very different forecasts for future development. The stunning regeneration of economic growth has encouraged upbeat readings of Russia's prospects, especially among many business leaders and economists. As President Putin approaches the end of his second term, Russia's society and its economy seem to be becoming, slowly and tentatively, more modern. By contrast, the recentralization of power and the decline of pluralism under President Putin generally lead those who follow political developments to very negative conclusions. Russian politics is moving further from the modern democratic mainstream.

Those who try to reconcile these divergent assessments find the bottom line, not surprisingly, somewhere in between. Yet contemporary Russia may be one of those rare cases in which the truth does not lie in the middle. The positive trends that are visible in Russia—primarily those involving economic and societal transformation—could, if properly encouraged, prove even more positive than generally recognized. And, although the negative trends of Russian politics are negative indeed, their potential ability to undermine even positive developments is, if anything, underestimated.

These divergent trends cannot usefully be reduced to a single bottom line. In politics, as in economics, the average is not always the right answer. The real question is how positive and negative developments interact with each other. Will the real opportunities created by growth be squandered as a result of bad policies that do not reduce Russia's overreliance on energy exports and that transform it into yet another of the world's corrupt "petro-states"? Will windfall energy earnings make Russia's "bureaucratic authoritarian" state too strong to challenge? Or will corruption and the state's inability to deal with the country's long-term problems provoke opposition within the elite and the public?

Russia's record of economic growth in the last half-decade provides some grounds for optimism about its long-term prospects. Nothing has done more to create a sense of confidence, normalcy, and new national possibilities.

- From 1991 to 1998, the contraction of Russia's gross domestic product (GDP) was almost 40 percent (and by some estimates, was even greater than that).

- Since 1999, the average annual growth of Russia's GDP has exceeded 6.5 percent—a record that, by the end of 2006, will have produced a cumulative economic expansion of 65 percent.

This record is often described as a story simply of high world prices for oil and other export commodities. There is no doubt that the price of oil (which has jumped from under $11 per barrel in 1998 to well over $60 per barrel in January 2006) has played the decisive role in Russia's turnaround—and that a drop in commodity prices would be devastating to the country's short-term economic prospects. Yet other factors have contributed to growth as well:

- Not only does Russia produce a commodity that commands a higher price than ever on world markets; it now produces much more of that commodity than it did the last decade. Daily production of oil, which had dropped to 5.85 million barrels per day in 1998, rebounded to more than 9 million barrels daily in 2005. In the past five years, the increase in Russian oil production has amounted to almost 50 percent of the worldwide increase.

- Russia's other exports have also risen. Export revenues of metals rose 61 percent in the last two years; of chemicals, 28 percent; of machinery and equipment, over 12 percent.

Growth has meant the steady improvement of Russian economic performance across the board, but nowhere more than in the area of fiscal stability.

- A government that was unable to manage its finances in the 1990s has now recorded five annual budget surpluses in a row. In 2005, government revenues exceeded spending by approximately 7 percent of GDP.

- Because of significant planned increases in spending for salaries, education, health, and housing, the surplus for 2006 is expected to drop to approximately 3.2 percent of GDP, but the option of addressing such social needs is one that did not even exist a decade ago.

- Today, the Russian state treasury holds hard-currency reserves of over $180 billion, and the Stabilization Fund, created in 2004 to capture windfall earnings from energy and save them for future needs, reached $50 billion by the beginning of 2006. It is not surprising that a government in such a situation can—as Russia recently did—issue thirty-year bonds on international markets.

Russia's new wealth has sparked a predictable debate about whether and how to spend it, and, as the plan to boost social expenditures in 2006 indicates, the pressure to enjoy the windfall has not been entirely resisted. Yet the amounts available are so great that increased spending has not kept the government from making significant improvements in its balance sheet. In 2004–2005, Russia made foreign debt payments of over $48 billion, including over $18 billion of early payments.

The contrast with Russia's desperate circumstances of a decade ago is striking, but perhaps the most consequential change has hardly been noticed: these choices are no longer being made in response to the demands and reproaches of other governments and international financial organizations. Disagreements on such matters often dominated Russia's relations with major Western countries in the 1990s. Today they no longer burden these relationships—they are, for the most part, no longer even discussed. To its own and others' relief, Russia makes these decisions—often wisely, sometimes not—on its own.

This transformation has been accompanied by a deeper integration of Russia into the international economy.

- Foreign direct investment in Russia, which totaled a mere $20 billion in the 1990s, was at least $16 billion in 2005 alone. Foreign funds have been a powerful reason for the strength of the Russian stock market, which was among the world's best-performing markets in 2005.

- Russian companies have also increased their own foreign investments. Lukoil, to take the best-known example, now owns more than two thousand retail and wholesale outlets selling gasoline in the United States.

- Six Russian stocks are now listed on the New York Stock Exchange, and more than thirty on the London exchange. To become eligible to be listed, and to be able to conduct public stock offerings, more Russian companies have adopted international standards of accounting and corporate transparency.

- The embrace of best practices goes beyond bookkeeping and annual reports. Russian businesses with Western partners, consultants, and technical advisers have introduced international management principles and strategies, increasing the productivity of the Russian economy.

- The prospect of Russian accession to the World Trade Organization (WTO) has further heightened awareness of the need to adjust to the competitive pressures and standards of a more open international economy.

Still more important to ordinary Russians are the signs that growth is having real trickle-down effects:

- Wage and pension arrears—a fact of post-Soviet life in the 1990s—have virtually disappeared.

- Between 2000 and 2004, the number of Russians living below the government's poverty line dropped from forty-two million to twenty-six million.

- The national unemployment rate—over 10 percent in 2000—is now about 7 percent.

- Economic growth has a broader regional base than is generally realized in the West. Moscow has a disproportionate share of national wealth, and nine of eighty-eight regions actually experienced negative growth in the first four years of recovery after 1998. Even so, the average growth of poorer regions exceeded 6 percent in this period.

Of special importance for the long-term spread and consolidation of democratic values and institutions, a middle class appears to be emerging. Measured by many Russian sociologists at approximately a quarter of society as a whole, it reflects changing consumption patterns, the confidence of those who for the first time in their lives own property, the expansion of small businesses, higher educational levels, greater travel opportunities, and—most significant—a mindset of new attitudes and expectations.

- Consumption, of course, leads these indicators. Moscow shopping centers have expanded tenfold since 1998. By 2002, the number of cars per one-hundred Russian households had tripled from 1990 (the last full year of the Soviet era), and the top foreign brand in 2004 was the distinctly down-market Hyundai.

- By 2000, Russia had 50 percent more college students than in 1992, and this number—as well as the number of colleges—has continued to grow.

- More than six million Russians traveled abroad in 2004 (up from under half a million annually at the beginning of the 1990s).

- Although the Russian public is often described as uninterested in politics and deferential to authority, poll results show attitudes much like those of other European countries. The respected Levada Center has found that 66 percent of Russians feel the country needs an effective political opposition and that 60 percent believe the media should be one of the forces playing such a role. For 57 percent, according to a December 2005 poll, media criticism of officials has only good results. (A mere 23 percent considered such criticism pointless.)

"Civil society" in its modern, Western sense depends, of course, on much more than middle-class consumption patterns or even middle-class attitudes and expectations. It involves the emergence and growth of autonomous social activities and organizations, and these too are very much in evidence in contemporary Russia. No single measure can capture this process of reinvigoration, which is occurring on many fronts.

- The variety, circulation, and financial self-sufficiency of Russian newspapers and magazines provide a contrast to the uniformity of the broadcast media.
- More than 700 million books—an estimated 90,000 titles—are published annually.
- Private business schools have appeared by the dozens and are now a preferred training ground for successful careers in the corporate sector.
- Twenty percent of Russians are regular Internet users, and use is higher still among the young.
- Corporate support of private charitable organizations grew sevenfold between 2000 and 2003, reaching $1.5 billion (ten times the amount now coming from foreign sources).
- Despite the oft-voiced fears of a decade ago about the collapse of Russian culture, the arts are experiencing a revival.
- Though nongovernmental organizations (NGOs) remain vulnerable (and their patriotic bona fides are challenged by the Kremlin), their numbers—in the hundreds of thousands, by some estimates—testify to a nascent civic consciousness that Russia has rarely known in the past.

These positive elements of Russia's ongoing transformation do not, of course, provide a complete picture of what is happening to the economy or society.

- The public health system is poor, and life expectancy continues to fall. According to the Russian Ministry of Health, Russia ranks 136th in the world in male life expectancy.
- According to President Putin himself, law-enforcement authorities can do nothing to prevent (or even account for) 70,000 Russian citizens who "disappear" every year. (Four years ago, he put the number of disappearances at 30,000.)
- The Chechen war appears to have metastasized into a far broader crisis of public disaffection and sporadic terrorism in the north Caucasus.

• Violent and organized xenophobia has gone beyond the garden-variety "skinhead-ism" encountered in many European societies, and Russian officials routinely mention it as a social ill for which they have developed no answer.

Many of these problems have deep historical and cultural roots, but to understand why the responses to them have been so weak and inadequate, we have to turn to the political transformation that has taken place in the past five years.

. . . And "De-Democratization"

The sustained growth record of the past half-decade has accelerated the transformation of Russia's economy and of its society, but this process is extremely fragile and its results still poorly consolidated. President Putin's advisers have frequently described their goal as the creation of a modern state, one that can protect and enlarge the benefits of social and economic change. They have no interest, they say, in returning to the obviously failed formulas of the Soviet system.

President Putin's sustained popularity has certainly given him the power and opportunity to steer Russia through a new phase of post-Soviet institution-building, and his tenure has had certain positive consequences. During his first term, economic liberalization acquired new momentum. And many citizens clearly derive satisfaction and confidence from having a capable national leader.

Yet taken as a whole the political balance sheet of the past five years is extremely negative. The practices and institutions that have developed over this period have become far less open, far less transparent, far less pluralist, far less subject to the rule of law, and far less vulnerable to the criticism and counterbalancing of a vigorous opposition or independent media. As the fifteen-year milestone of the Soviet Union's breakup approaches, Russia—almost alone among European countries—is actually moving further away from modern European political norms.

Russia's political evolution in this decade is often explained as a corrective to its evolution in the previous one. At the end of the 1990s, there was a strong consensus within the elite and more broadly within society that the disorderly post-Soviet transformation of Russian politics under President Boris Yeltsin had taken a heavy toll on the credibility and effectiveness of state institutions, and that the state needed a significant cleanup and reinvigoration—in some instances even complete rebuilding. From extortion and harassment by petty officials to vast fortunes created by the appropriation of state assets, the legacy of the 1990s plainly called for a new broom and for honest and activist political leadership. President Putin appealed to such sentiments when he promised to create the rule—even, as he put it, the "dictatorship"—of law, when he proposed to limit the bureaucratic harassment that obliged ordinary citizens and small-business owners to pay unending bribes, and when he spoke of breaking the political power of Yeltsin-era "oligarchs."

Five years later, however, Russian institutions are almost universally seen as more corrupt than in the past.

- In last year's rankings of 117 countries by the World Economic Forum, Russia fell from 85th place to 106th in "favoritism in decisions of government officials," from 84th to 102nd in "judicial independence," and from 88th to 108th in "protection of property rights."

- In parallel 2005 rankings of corruption by Transparency International, Russia placed 126th out of 159 countries and was tied—with Belarus—for the largest negative change.

- A survey of more than 2,000 respondents by the Information Science for Democracy (INDEM) Fund, conducted by Georgi Satarov and other Russian researchers, concluded that between 2001 and 2005, the average bribe that Russian businesses had to pay increased by 70 percent and that the total "corruption market" was more than 2.5 times larger than the federal budget.

- Anecdotal impressions confirm these findings. Numerous American business people have told members of this Task Force that, although foreign companies are less endangered by organized crime than they were in the past, they now face "the real mafia . . . the state."

- Official government figures also emphasize the lack of enforcement of laws and regulations on the books. The Interior Ministry estimates, to take one small example, that 75 percent of seafood exported from the Russian Far East is illegal, as are half of Russian roundwood timber exports.

Corruption is not merely a matter of coerced taxation on businesses and individuals or of illicit payments that subvert public policy. After the most shocking week of terrorism in modern Russia—the hijacking of two airliners by suicide bombers and the attack on the school in Beslan in September 2004—it became known that the terrorists had made their way to their targets by paying small bribes to law-enforcement officials.

The most consequential single episode in the refashioning of the Russian state in this decade occurred at the intersection of politics and economics. The so-called Khodorkovsky affair involved the forced breakup of Russia's largest private oil company, Yukos, and the long-term imprisonment of its top officials on charges of tax evasion. Too little is reliably known about the motives behind the targeting of Mikhail Khodorkovsky to say much about what the case reveals about President Putin's long-term vision of the Russian state. Its impact, however, is easy to describe. For all its drama, the move to break up Yukos did not represent a full reconsideration of the privatizations of the 1990s, nor did it put in place a new and settled consensus with clear rules. It was a case tailored to one man and one company, and the main precedent it established is that anyone can become vulnerable when the state bureaucracy, either at the president's direction or merely with his support, decides to seize private assets.

The break-up of Yukos and the acquisition by the state of additional major pieces of the oil industry mean that the Russian energy sector is now increasingly not just state-owned but Kremlin-controlled. The factional politics of the presidential administration has immediate consequences for energy output, licensing decisions, pipeline routes, etc. Russia is left more vulnerable to what President Putin's then–chief economic adviser last year called "Venezuelan disease"—a syndrome in which nationalization is followed by slower growth, inept management, and official malfeasance.

The competition for power and influence in Russian politics has become a struggle over how to share personal ownership of vast natural-resource wealth (and recently the effort to restore state control of "strategic" assets of the economy has been extended to other sectors as well). To become a high official of the Kremlin is to become a part-owner of some of the world's largest corporations; to lose one's official post means a potentially gigantic loss of personal wealth, or worse.

Greater Kremlin control of the "commanding heights" of the Russian economy would have had a completely different meaning in an economy that was more diversified and in a political system that was strengthening legality and creating institutional checks on the abuse of power. It might have meant only less-effective corporate management and possibly slower growth. Had it really strengthened the rule of law, it might in time have even paved the way for a resurgent pluralism.

Instead, at every level of Russian politics, the dominant trend of the past five years has been in the opposite direction—toward the erosion of pluralism and more arbitrary and unregulated exercise of state power. This has been true of relations between the branches of government, between center and periphery, between the government and the media, between government and civil society, and between those who wield political power and those who command economic resources.

As a result, other political institutions are no longer able to operate as a true counterweight to presidential power.

- The lower house of Russia's parliament, the Duma, in which fewer parties have been able to gain seats either by qualifying for proportional representation or by winning elections in single-mandate districts, is now controlled by the president's party, United Russia.

- The upper house of parliament, once made up of regional governors, is now composed of presidential appointees, and the governors themselves are now selected by the president.

- The recent restructuring of the judiciary has strengthened the subordination of Russia's courts to executive power.

- Control of the electoral process has also been tightened, making it more difficult to mount a challenge of any kind to the ruling party. Representation in parliament will in the future be open only to parties that cross a threshold of 7 percent, compared to 5 percent in the past; no seats will be awarded in single-mandate districts.

- Similarly, the law on elections passed in 2005 makes it harder to form a party, prohibits the formation of electoral blocs between parties, and outlaws election monitoring by independent domestic organizations (which, unlike international monitors, can mobilize human resources on a scale needed for a comprehensive assessment).

- The Kremlin has been able to establish near-exclusive authority over the flow of funds during electoral campaigns. Influential Russians claim that contributions not approved by the presidential staff invite a visit from the tax police.

It is a revealing measure of the impact of these changes that in the last two parliamentary campaigns, only two new parties have been able to gain proportional-representation seats in the Duma, and both of these are widely understood to have been created by the Kremlin.

Russia's wealth has greatly expanded the resources available for political activity, but control over who receives them has been dramatically narrowed. This pattern is not limited to party politics. Just as it created the new "opposition" nationalist party Rodina (Motherland), the Kremlin has sponsored the youth group Nashi (Ours), also with a nationalist platform. Its organizers have openly described their strategy as one of preempting the formation of authentically independent movements. The same anti-pluralist strategy was evident in the draft law on NGOs, first passed in November 2005 and then in amended form a month later. A storm of international criticism removed some of the restrictions that were to have been placed on foreign NGOs operating in Russia, but the final version preserved the more important goal of keeping domestic NGOs under new controls and registration requirements, and restricted their access to foreign resources.

While the print media retain some diversity, the Kremlin limits political debate and competition by carefully controlling the broadcast media on which most Russians rely for news and entertainment. Five years ago, when a weak economy—and limited advertising revenues—threatened to make TV unprofitable, the state managed to seize control of NTV, Russia's only independent national network. Subsequent efforts kept other channels out of the hands of those who opposed (or might at some point in the future oppose) the current political leadership.

Today, economic growth and modern technology mean that new channels keep appearing, but close administrative control prevents any of them from becoming a major source of alternative news programming or a platform allowing opposition parties and candidates broad public exposure during political campaigns.

Russian officials frequently point out that this or that measure of political tightening introduced by President Putin can also be found in a Western country that is a stable and respected democracy. This is correct, but meaningless. Russia stands alone in applying such measures across the board. Under President Putin, power has been centralized and pluralism reduced in every single area of politics. As a result, Russia is left only with the trappings of democratic rule—their form, but not their content.

At the time of the presidential transition from Yeltsin to Putin, some Russians believed that the streamlining of state institutions might make it easier to deal with the many problems that had been left unaddressed, or even made worse, in the 1990s. Five years later, the opposite seems closer to the truth. The elimination of meaningful pluralism has become one of the most significant obstacles to addressing the unfinished business of post-Soviet reconstruction.

High levels of corruption, ineffective institutions, and the centralization of power, along with the need to observe at least superficially democratic forms—all these factors also make it difficult to predict the evolution of the Russian political system when President Putin leaves office in 2008. Although Putin's continuing popularity is not in doubt, his successor is unlikely to enjoy the same kind of public support or be able to block the emergence of factional divisions within the elite. Lacking the legitimacy that Putin enjoys as the presumed architect of growth and "stability" since the 1990s, a successor may—especially in the event of an economic downturn—face a choice between opening the system up and further tightening political controls. President Putin has successfully centralized power for his own use, but he has not created the institutions—least of all, representative institutions—that could be expected to shape and stabilize Russian politics in the future. As a result, the range of imaginable outcomes is uncomfortably wide.

U.S.-Russian Relations Today

The end of the Cold War left the United States with the challenge of creating a new relationship with Russia, the largest and most important of the Soviet successor states. Since then, three presidents have grappled with this problem, and although their responses differed in ways that reflected the specific issues before them, all recognized that productive relations with Russia were one of the highest priorities of American foreign policy.

- All three aimed to leave nuclear and ideological rivalry behind and to build relations between Moscow and Washington on a solid foundation of compatible national interests.

- Each sought to lubricate bilateral cooperation by expanding trade and enlarging Russia's role in the international frameworks and forums from which it had been excluded during the Cold War.

- They recognized that Russia's post-revolutionary adjustment to the modern world—the building of new political, social, and economic institutions—would be gradual.

- And all three treated good personal relations with Russia's leaders as a valuable lever for increasing cooperation and solving problems.

The Post–September 11 Partnership

American hopes for productive relations with Russia reached their peak in the immediate aftermath of September 11, 2001. Bush administration policymakers believed—and outside experts tended to agree—that conditions were favorable for the development of a strong and lasting partnership that would help the United States deal effectively with new and acute threats to national security. Moscow and Washington had never been closer in their reading of global dangers. The issues at the top of each side's international agenda—Islamist terrorism, nuclear proliferation, and energy—seemed, for once, to be the same. And the United States, for a change, actively wanted Russia to join in meeting these threats, not merely to stay out of the way.

In this new and positive context, disagreements were not expected to disappear, but they were expected to be more manageable. Frictions of the recent past—over the enlargement of the North Atlantic Treaty Organization (NATO) or national missile defense, or over Russia's internal politics or its policy toward its post-Soviet neighbors—would not be allowed to derail cooperation on matters of high priority to both sides.

Russia's new leadership played a key role in supporting these optimistic expectations. As president, Putin seemed to combine (as Yeltsin had not since the earliest days of his tenure) overwhelming domestic popularity with a personal commitment to be part of the West.

U.S.-Russian relations did enjoy a vigorous resurgence in this period. Agreement on how to deal with terrorism, nuclear proliferation, and global energy needs seemed particularly strong.

- The American campaign in Afghanistan benefited from the sharing of Russian intelligence information as well as from access to Central Asian military airfields, which Russia did not seek to block. Russian officials welcomed the United States as a new recruit to an effort—fighting Islamist terrorism—that they had long championed. For his part, President George W. Bush referred to Russia as an "ally" in the struggle.

- The United States led the effort at the 2002 summit of the G8 in Canada to create the $20 billion Global Partnership against the Spread of Weapons and Materials of Mass Destruction to improve the security of dangerous, especially fissionable, materials. Russia also became part of the U.S.-proposed Proliferation Security Initiative, a multinational network to interdict such materials.

- Russia also joined multilateral diplomatic talks on North Korea's nuclear weapons program, reacted negatively in 2002 to revelations of secret Iranian nuclear activities, and offered support for the efforts of the United Kingdom, France, and Germany to negotiate a suspension of key elements of Iran's nuclear activities.

- At their Moscow summit in June 2002, Presidents Bush and Putin launched a "strategic energy dialogue," with the aim of increasing coordination and contact among energy officials as well as companies. An early offshoot was the project, announced by a consortium of Russian companies, to build a privately owned pipeline to Murmansk to facilitate oil exports to the United States.

This surge in relations hardly involved complete agreement, and, in fact, on the most divisive international issue of the period—Iraq—Russia supported France and Germany in threatening to block the American effort to win United Nations (UN) Security Council approval of military action. Yet Presidents Putin and Bush were broadly successful in blunting the impact of this and other disagreements that might have jeopardized an enhanced partnership.

- They papered over their differences on the abrogation of the Anti-Ballistic Missile (ABM) Treaty and signed a strategic arms-reduction treaty. Its few details and minimal verification provisions reflected the lower priority that the Bush administration assigned to arms control; the fact that there was a treaty at all reflected successful Russian lobbying for a formal agreement, however minimal. On each side, confidence that the risk of nuclear confrontation had essentially disappeared made the details of an agreement seem unimportant.

- Russian officials signaled that their neighbors' efforts to integrate with the West had become a more manageable concern for them. The United States supported—and Russia accepted—an invitation to upgrade relations between Russia and NATO through the formation of the NATO-Russia Council, a body with a new mandate to make security cooperation work. When the time came for NATO to issue invitations to the Baltic states to become members, the Russian response was muted. And President Putin actually explained in public why American training of Georgian military personnel contributed to Russian security.

* Even the war in Chechnya—on which the two sides did not agree— became easier to manage as a bilateral issue. President Bush spoke sympathetically of the terrorist threat that Russia faced there, and President Putin expressed his commitment to a political settlement.

The ability to see concrete problems in the same light and to work effectively in dealing with them was crucial in cementing a U.S.-Russian partnership in this period. Yet a psychological transformation— on both sides—seemed no less important. President Putin came to be seen by many Americans—especially those with whom he dealt regularly—as an effective modernizer, determined to make his country work better as it tackled a large backlog of unaddressed problems. A series of reformist legislative measures early in his first term gave credence to the idea that the rule of law was taking hold. To some Western observers, the fine points of Putin's democratic vision seemed un-knowable and possibly beside the point. His commitment to moving his country into the international mainstream seemed, by contrast, obvious. At the same time, polls showed that many Russians, who increasingly felt that their own country was on a more hopeful track, began in turn to view the United States more favorably. The drama of September 11 and its aftermath had done more than demonstrate the need for cooperation. Russia had for over a decade been on the receiving end of American ideas and assistance. Now it seemed that a partnership might be forged on more equal terms.

The Recent Record

The passage of time has undone much of the transformation of U.S.-Russian relations that followed September 11. This erosion occurred even on issues that had been thought to involve a strong strategic con-sensus.

In 2005, Russian officials sought to curtail access by the United States and NATO to Central Asian air bases—even though these were still being used to support military and humanitarian operations in

Afghanistan, an effort that Russia ostensibly supported. For the first time since 2001, Moscow prepared to throw up obstacles to Western policy, not because it now disagreed with the goal of fighting terrorism, but because it subordinated this goal to a different, geopolitical concern. Acting in the framework of the Shanghai Cooperation Organization (the other members of which are Central Asian states), Russia and China saw an opportunity to reverse the growing American presence in the region.

American hopes for expanded energy cooperation also encountered a series of disappointments: the revocation of long-standing ExxonMobil licenses for Sakhalin natural gas fields; the destruction of Russia's largest and best-managed oil company, Yukos, as part of the reassertion of state control over the oil sector; the enunciation of new policies to limit Western investment in Russian energy development; the delay and near-collapse of the Murmansk pipeline project; and the cutoff of gas to Ukraine and, beyond it, to the rest of Europe, as part of a counterattack against Kiev's pro-Western orientation. Under the cumulative impact of these developments, the "strategic energy dialogue" came to a standstill.

Of the three issues that gave the post–September 11 relationship real meaning—counterterrorism, energy security, and nonproliferation—only the last remains an example of truly robust cooperation. In the past six months, Russia has had to balance two competing interests: on the one hand, good relations with Tehran (which include sharply increased military sales and the goal of further sales of nuclear power reactors), and on the other, maintaining solidarity with Western states in an effort to keep Iran from becoming a nuclear-weapons state. Facing this choice, Russia's coordination of policy with the West has actually grown stronger. Moscow has dismissed suggestions that political, economic, or other sanctions might have to be imposed on Tehran, but it has supported efforts to refer the issue of Iran's nuclear activities to the UN Security Council. It has also pursued a parallel proposal, with U.S. and European encouragement, to provide nuclear-enrichment services so as to head off the further development of Iran's own capabilities in this area.

Tentative cooperation in dealing with Iran is especially noteworthy because it has occurred as the tone of U.S.-Russian relations on other issues has deteriorated. Foremost among these has been Russia's escalating concern about the loss of influence in its own neighborhood. The so-called "color revolutions"—popular demonstrations challenging electoral fraud in the former Soviet states—usually resulted in the accession to power of leaders determined to accelerate their integration into the West. Despite their own substantial efforts to influence these events (and the investment of resources on a large scale), Russian leaders have increasingly found subversive and anti-Russian purposes in U.S. democracy-promotion programs.

NATO enlargement has also reemerged as a contentious issue, and not simply because some former Soviet states have expressed a desire to follow the Baltic states as new members. Although the alliance's accession offers to Estonia, Latvia, and Lithuania in 2002 had evoked only routine negative comments from Moscow, by 2004, Defense Minister Sergei Ivanov declared that their full integration into NATO defenses might result in a reconsideration of Russian nuclear strategy.

Despite the Bush administration's apparent desire to keep the issue of democratic change from becoming a prominent issue of bilateral relations, President Bush and other senior officials have gradually changed course on this question. The place of democracy in American foreign policy dominated the president's second inaugural address, and one month later it also apparently dominated the agenda of his first second-term meeting with President Putin in Bratislava. Since then, Russian officials have frequently complained about administration statements linking the president's "freedom agenda" in any way to relations with Russia.

Finally, the personal outlook of policymakers on both sides has changed, making possible statements that would have been unthinkable even a year or two earlier. Secretary of State Condoleezza Rice's reproach of Russia for its cutoff of gas to Ukraine was one such example. Far more revealing and significant, however, were the comments of President Putin after the Beslan school murders of 2004. Despite worldwide expressions of sympathy, his own speech to the Russian people appeared to blame the United States for what had happened. In a remark showing the distance traveled since September 11, he said that terrorists trying to destroy Russia had been aided by unnamed foreign supporters who believed "that Russia still remains one of the world's nuclear powers and as such represents a threat to them. And so they reason that this threat should be removed."

Findings 1: Partnership, Selective Cooperation, or . . . ?

Russian and American leaders have for many years used the hopeful term "partnership"—and often the still grander one, "strategic partnership"—to describe their vision for relations between Moscow and Washington. Reality has, with brief exceptions, usually been more modest. Russia and the United States have only very rarely acted as partners in any meaningful sense of the word. When they have cooperated, it has been because their interests on this or that narrow issue were sufficiently similar to allow them to work together. But cumulative effects—an accretion of trust, the habit of joint action, a spillover to other issues—have been few.

What would a genuine U.S.-Russian partnership require? It would go beyond similar assessments of specific international problems and opportunities.

- It would rest on a conviction that, while great nations have their differences on specific issues, their strategic interests are so similar that neither has to fear—or seek to undermine—the other.

- It would be strengthened by mutual confidence that the other side is willing to commit resources to deal with new challenges, that its institutions can be counted on to perform effectively, and that disagreements will be addressed through candid discussion and are not the expression of unspoken goals and resentments.

29

- Strong common interest would lie at the heart of such a relationship, but only a strong common outlook would make it succeed.

Looked at in this light, U.S.-Russian relations are clearly far from meeting the conditions of authentic partnership. For the foreseeable future it will be all but impossible to put relations on such a footing. The mutual confidence that partnership requires is missing. When Russia and the United States work together it is likely to be a matter of case-by-case, carefully circumscribed cooperation.

For this, the requirements are much less demanding:

- Each side has to believe that working together on a given problem is on balance a plus; it does not need to believe in any broad convergence of interests. Each side should want to understand the other side's views as best it can, but it need not share them.

- Cooperation in one case does not necessarily make cooperation in the next more likely. Even when circumstances seem to call for collaboration, each side may remain wary of the other's reliability, of hidden bureaucratic agendas, or of a desire to seek one-sided advantage.

Over the next two to three years, the U.S.-Russian relationship will often seem like two different relationships, based on different principles and expectations. On the high-priority issue of Iran, cooperation may continue; on other issues, increased disagreement and rivalry are likely.

The list of factors that can negatively shape the relationship is too long to justify any other forecast:

- The Russian electoral calendar means that the political tightening of the recent past has probably not run its full course. President Putin and his advisers are leaving much less to chance than Boris Yeltsin did as he approached the end of his second term in 1999, and their approach will keep dramatizing Russia's status outside the mainstream of modern democratic politics.

- Russia's policies toward virtually all its neighbors are increasingly animated by a spirit of competition with the West in general and with the United States in particular, and by a greater willingness to jeopardize cooperation with both the United States and major European states. Though several episodes have now cast Moscow in the worst possible light, this approach continues. It seems to guide Russian policy toward the so-called "frozen conflicts"—unresolved separatist conflicts in other post-Soviet states. In several of these, Russia is the principal source of external support for separatist forces. (Russian officials, moreover, have warned that if final-status talks lead to independence for Kosovo, they may support independence for breakaway jurisdictions in neighboring states.)

- Russian energy policy has turned a prized asset of economic relations into a potential tool of political intimidation. Russian officials make no secret of their belief that their country's commanding position in world energy markets should help advance its political objectives. The cutoff of gas supplies to Ukraine has been the most shocking and coercive application of this view to date, but others may lie ahead.

- Increasing sales of arms and advanced military technologies to China—and Russo-Chinese efforts to make small gains at American expense—mean a growing divergence between Russian policy, on the one hand, and U.S. and European policy, on the other. With last year's large-scale military exercises, this gap has become even wider.

- Russia faces what one of President Putin's senior political advisers calls an "underground fire" in the North Caucasus—made worse by the unending war in Chechnya—and its vulnerability to major terrorist incidents in that region and across Russia remains high. A problem that ought to encourage U.S.-Russian cooperation is made divisive by Moscow's preference for blaming outsiders—even the West—and by its embrace of repressive strategies elsewhere in the former Soviet Union.

A relationship that has to deal with a list of problems like this one is more likely to get worse than it is to get better. If so, American policy will face the challenge of trying to deal with three very different kinds of problems.

- First, the United States needs to do more to promote cooperation with Russia on those issues where the cost of not working together is especially high and a constructive result remains a realistic possibility.

- Second, where Russian policy is becoming less positive, the United States needs a response that recognizes the change and adjusts to it. American policy has to explore expanded cooperation on issues where Russia is prepared to make itself part of the solution, but it cannot count on hopes for cooperation in those cases where Russia has become part of the problem.

- Finally, there are issues where the gap between the U.S. approach and that of Russia has become so wide that cooperation is unlikely and where good results can be achieved only by drawing a clearer line between U.S. interests and values and those reflected in current Russian policy.

American policy toward Russia has to become more selective, and the approach the United States selects will vary from issue to issue. Iran and nuclear security are prime examples of problems in the first of the three categories above—issues of vital national-security importance where effective U.S.-Russian cooperation can be facilitated by an expanded effort.

- On issues like Iran and the security of dangerous nuclear materials, Russia has shown strong, sometimes even resentful sensitivity to American efforts to shape its policies and practices, but it has also revealed an underlying common interest that makes joint action possible.

- In both of these cases, there is little—or, in the case of nuclear security, no—chance of getting a satisfactory result without Russian participation.

The United States needs a different approach for dealing with problems in the second category, in which potential common interests may be giving way to greater discord. Energy security is one such issue.

- Energy cooperation with Russia was once seen as a new and direct route to increased global energy security, but it has now become an area of tension as well. An effective policy needs to reflect both these realities.

- True energy security can be advanced by increased Western participation in the development of Russia's vast resources. At the same time, it is inconsistent with a system of corporate governance that makes Russia's strategic resources a day-to-day political tool to be used by Kremlin officials. This system makes politically motivated energy cut-offs a permanent possibility and makes it impossible to treat Russia's state-owned companies as though they were commercial entities.

• The United States cannot expect Russian energy policy to substitute for its own. If America and its allies lack a comprehensive strategy to increase supplies of energy, diversify the number of suppliers and transport routes, and promote energy efficiency, they will only increase Russia's ability to exploit its market position for political purposes.

Russia's relations with China may also need to be included in this second category of issues, in which common and clashing interests both play a role.

• Like the United States and other leading states, Russia has an interest in relating its economic future to the expanding Chinese market. No American interest is challenged by this or by good Russo-Chinese relations in general.

• Yet how Russia intends to relate its future security strategy to China's expanding power is a question with more dangerous potential, including for U.S.-Russian relations. Recent signs of Russo-Chinese cooperation against the United States—above all, the seeming readiness of Russia and China to subordinate joint action against terrorism to geopolitical rivalry—represent a small but unmistakable warning sign of future international alignments.

• The cooperative atmosphere that now characterizes relations among the leading powers has no greater potential benefit than the possibility of managing China's integration into international politics on terms that serve peace, prosperity and freedom. A Russian strategy that encouraged rather than restrained China in disagreements with the United States and major regional states would make such a positive outcome less likely.

Finally, there are those problems on which American policy needs to recognize how sharp the differences between U.S. interests and policies and Russia's have, unfortunately, become. Here we refer to two issues—Russia's relations with its neighbors and the growing authoritarianism of its political institutions. Neither of these is a new issue in U.S.-Russian relations, but in the past the two sides have generally been able to avoid dealing with them directly and divisively. Now latent disagreement has become more open and destructive, and the two issues have become intertwined.

- Russian officials and commentators accuse the West of sponsoring mass demonstrations and movements—"color revolutions"—in the former Soviet states. Behind the ostensible purpose of these protests—to guarantee free and fair elections—they claim to discern a broader design: to destabilize the Russian periphery; to claim new members for NATO; and to encircle, weaken, and perhaps even dismember Russia.

- For Kremlin officials, concern about organized popular politics in neighboring states is clearly not just a matter of geopolitics. "Color revolutions" seem to represent the possibility of a challenge to their own power and position—and an opportunity to push for new measures of political control within Russia.

Findings 2: Democracy and Integration

In fashioning its policy toward Russia over the next half-decade, the United States clearly has to address a very full agenda—from problems where the two sides still operate on the basis of broadly similar assessments to those where disagreements have come close to preventing reasonable discussion. Of all these, no issue has created greater confusion both at home and abroad than that of how democracy fits into American policy as a whole. The United States needs to explain more clearly and consistently why the advancing authoritarianism of Russian politics is a legitimate American concern and how it may affect U.S. policy toward Russia and other post-Soviet states.

All the many reasons that can be brought to bear for why the United States should care about the state of Russian democracy do not mean that it is the only thing that the United States cares about, nor that it will always be the most important thing. Terrorism and Iran's nuclear ambitions, for example, are currently of great concern to U.S. policymakers. Although President Putin is presiding over the rollback of Russian democracy, the United States should obviously work with him to keep Iran from acquiring nuclear weapons and to keep terrorists from attacking either his country or ours. President Putin has not suggested that he will do so only as long as the United States pretends that he is a champion of Russian democracy. Russia cooperates with the United States on Iran to advance its own interests, and will continue to do so unless it comes to see its interests differently.

Yet even if there is no need to make sharp trade-offs between such concerns, Washington must be able to say why it takes an interest in Russia's domestic evolution in the first place. This is particularly necessary because some Russians appear to believe that what the United States advocates is either deeply unrealistic or deeply cynical and that it does so because it does not understand Russia and its problems or because it aims to weaken Russia and prevent its revival as a great power.

In fact, the importance that American policy attaches to modern democratic institutions in all post-Soviet states is a practical as well as a principled concern.

- Russian authoritarians try to cast themselves as protectors of stable and effective government. Yet Russians are discovering—both from daily experience and from national tragedies—that corrupt bureaucracies cannot deal successfully with terrorism, reform the armed forces, manage efficient energy companies, keep the police from harassing ordinary citizens, create a regulatory framework that encourages the growth of small business, or even do much about the drug trade or organized crime. Above all, they cannot reform themselves.

- They are even less likely to perform these functions if they can keep television from reporting on their performance, are never investigated by parliament, do not report to political leaders who have to win genuinely contested elections, and can manipulate the electoral system to insulate themselves from oversight. No rhetoric about creating a strong and effective state can substitute for these mechanisms.

Democratic legitimacy will also play a role in the stability of other post-Soviet states besides Russia.

- The politics of these countries will not always be limited to a contest between the corrupt state bureaucracies that now dominate so many of them and their democratic challengers. In some of these states Islamist radicals and even varieties of fascism will bid for power.

- American policy assumes—correctly—that governments trying to turn back extremist challenges will need the extra strength, and the broad base, that democratic processes confer.

- When Russia's leaders encourage the reactionary strategies of other post-Soviet governments, they are raising—not lowering—the long-term risk of extremism and instability in their own neighborhood.

Even with its rapidly increasing wealth, Russia itself will not truly be strengthened by authoritarianism. Authoritarianism will block the modernization of Russia's institutions and keep them weak. Over the long term, President Putin's policies can be no more successful than the institutions that support them and implement them. On their current course, therefore, they are likely to fail; they will limit rather than accelerate Russian growth, and—of greatest significance for Americans—they will make it harder for the United States to treat Russia as a capable prospective partner.

A realistic American policy cannot, of course, be based on the illusion that democratic governance can take hold in a large and complex country such as Russia unless there is a genuine and organized popular desire for it. Only the Russian people can, over time, identify the institutions and leaders that will serve them best.

- The experience of the 1990s taught Western policymakers about the psychological and political traps of assistance relationships, and there is no reason to regret the fact that the West has less economic leverage over Russia's decisions than it used to.

- The fact that Russia no longer has a desperate need for external assistance is healthy. At the same time, it may lead Russia's leaders to believe that they can safely defer the creation of modern representative institutions capable of dealing with the country's real problems.

- For this reason, the few purposes for which the United States should continue to offer assistance to Russia in the future, in addition to nuclear security, humanitarian relief, public health, and people-to-people exchanges, include support for a free and fair democratic process.

It is sometimes said—critically—that there is not much that the United States can do about the advance of authoritarianism in Russia, other than talk about it. We agree, but we believe that it needs to do at least this much—consistently and forcefully. How Western leaders talk about democracy can make a difference. Just last year, for example, loud international criticism led to changes in draft legislation regulating the activities of Russian NGOs.

In talking about these and other issues, the United States needs to pay particular attention to building a consensus with its European allies. Americans and Europeans have too often differed in the emphasis they put on this or that dimension of Russian policy. Whenever they disagreed the result was the same—making it easier for Russian leaders to dismiss Western criticisms.

This is now changing. Because the authoritarian trend in Russia is such a broad one, and because it intersects with negative trends in Russian foreign policy, American and European assessments are converging. This is the moment to cement a consensus. The West's policy toward Iran in the past two years shows the importance of unity: Russia has seen that the costs of isolating itself would be greater than they would be if it were dealing with complaints from only one country.

- A transatlantic consensus will also raise Kremlin anxieties about its international standing. By contrast, intermittent and isolated protests about negative internal trends will have little impact.

- Only when the United States and Europe express joint objections to Russia's policy toward its neighbors is Moscow likely to believe that these will be reinforced by real resources and political will.

- Western unity sends an important message to Russians beyond the Kremlin as well. Russian energy companies have been counting on European markets to drive their future growth; nothing will more meaningfully demonstrate to them the adverse impact of their own government's actions than to see the United States and its allies working together to diversify energy supplies away from Russia.

The most important reason that the United States needs to create a consensus with its European allies on policy toward Russia is that the single issue that may matter most to Moscow is one that it will take seriously only if it sees a united Western approach. This is the question of Russia's integration into the global "clubs" in which the leading powers try to forge a consensus about how to deal with common political, security, and economic problems. In the last ten years, Russia has achieved an impressive measure of integration into these international frameworks, but it is by no means complete and should not be irreversible. The United States and Europe should convince Russia's leaders that ground that has been won can also be lost.

Russia's authoritarian direction has led some to call for its suspension from the G8. This is not our view: We favor keeping Russia in the G8, but its recent conduct makes it a much closer call than we expected. A country that has in the space of a single year supported massive fraud in the elections of its largest European neighbor and then punished it for voting wrong by turning off its gas supply has to be at least on informal probation at a meeting of the world's industrial democracies.

- If the decision to hold the G8 summit in St. Petersburg were being made today, it would obviously have to be made differently.

- Yet even if the issue of Russia's chairmanship is not reopened, the discussion agenda of the meeting must not ignore Russia's conduct. When the G8 members discuss energy security, they have to discuss it in its fullest sense, including the ways in which Russia has undermined it.

- They must not, moreover, discuss energy security alone. Over the longer term, a Russia that does not share the norms of the G8 threatens to make that institution much less useful for its other members.

- To prevent this result, the democratic members of the G8—the United States and its allies—need to reconstitute the old G7, as a guiding and coordinating force within the group. Even with Russia's inclusion in the G8, the G7 has continued to meet to discuss certain financial issues; selected political questions now require a similar format.

There is a useful lesson in the fact that Russia's chairmanship of the G8 comes just as doubts about its suitability even to be a member are also rising: If integration is merely a gesture of political friendship, it is less likely to achieve its intended result. In general, we hope that Russia qualifies to participate in such organizations, but if it does not qualify, it should not become a member.

In the near term, this lesson has special relevance for Russia's negotiations to join the WTO.

- We strongly favor accession, but on this condition: It must not be a political present (least of all on the eve of a G8 summit that Russia is chairing as a result of another political present). The WTO has an important role in international trade that should not be degraded in this way.

- Accession should mean that Russia accepts and will abide by the norms of a rule-based trading system. If Moscow sees that it has been admitted for political reasons, it will have less reason to play by the rules.

Looking over the horizon, the United States and its allies should also examine the advantages and disadvantages of perpetuating the NATO-Russia Council.

- This consultative body was created with special status in the aftermath of September 11, in large part to ease Russian concerns over the pending round of NATO enlargement. Allaying resentment is not, however, a strong basis for cooperation if it is not at the same time reinforced by common interests. Integration on a weak foundation simply produces empty multilateral mechanisms that do not work as well as they should.

- Over the long term, the existence of the NATO-Russia Council needs to be justified on terms that parallel NATO membership. Its members should be committed to democratic principles, share a common perspective on major security issues, and be ready and able to cooperate to meet common challenges.

Russia's integration into the leading international frameworks is not merely a matter of status and prestige. Its participation is valuable if it broadens the number of major powers working together to address common challenges and thereby increases their chances of success. The United States has favored—and should continue to favor—Russia's inclusion. But its integration, to have genuinely positive results, needs a strong foundation. Fifteen years after the end of the Cold War, that foundation is far weaker than it should be.

Recommendations 1: Security

Every major category of U.S.-Russian relations—military security, economics, politics—includes issues on which cooperation can bring important benefits to the United States, others on which the potential benefit seems to be declining, and still others on which Russia and the United States are increasingly at odds. The challenge for U.S. policymakers in the future is to design and implement policies that serve U.S. interests no matter how much cooperation they actually achieve.

Nonproliferation and Nuclear Cooperation

The United States must expand its cooperation with Russia to keep the most dangerous international actors from acquiring the most dangerous weapons, technologies, and materials. This is a fundamental American security interest—one that is far easier to protect if Washington and Moscow work together and far harder if they do not.

No aspect of this problem will require greater attention for the foreseeable future than Iran's expanding nuclear activities.

- As the only major power that engages in nuclear cooperation with Iran, Russia could play a pivotal role in creating a framework that restrains these activities. Its agreement with Iran to take spent fuel from the Bushehr reactor back to Russia as well as its proposal to enrich uranium in Russia for Iranian reactors indicate Moscow's readiness to play a constructive role.

- Russia is also the only power that can effectively threaten Iran with nuclear isolation if it continues to build sensitive nuclear fuel-cycle facilities.

The United States should not approach this problem as one to be solved by side-deals and payoffs. If Russian and American strategic assessments converge, then policymakers on both sides will have a continuing reason to cooperate even while disagreeing on other issues. If Russian and American policies are not based on the same strategic assessment, no deal between Moscow and Washington is likely to last.

Although it should not be necessary to "buy" Russian support, successful cooperation does have to rest on mutual confidence, and this sentiment can be strengthened by updating the policies of both countries toward Iran and by a stronger framework for cooperation on nuclear issues in general.

- American objections to Russia's Bushehr reactor project and other Russian nuclear cooperation with Iran have in the past prevented the negotiation of a general framework for bilateral U.S.-Russian cooperation on civilian nuclear energy issues—a so-called 123 agreement (required by section 123 of the Atomic Energy Act). The United States should now recognize explicitly what has been implicit in its position for some time: that a Russian policy that limits nuclear cooperation with Iran to nonsensitive technologies would justify dropping our historic objections to the Bushehr reactor.

- For its part, Russia needs to accept what it has never recognized, either explicitly or implicitly: that the international community may soon face an Iran so determined to produce fissile material that all nuclear cooperation between Moscow and Tehran, including the Bushehr reactor, should cease. Russian acceptance of this view will be a litmus test for expanded U.S.-Russian cooperation.

- Russia wants the United States to accept Russian projects that do not contribute to Iran's fuel-cycle capabilities, and it makes sense to do so. But Russia needs to make clear to Iran that its conduct puts all nuclear cooperation with other countries at risk.

A "123 agreement" will allow expanded cooperation on many fronts—including the Bush administration's own Global Nuclear

Energy Partnership Initiative. Such cooperation would reflect Russia's status as a major factor in nuclear commerce, from fuel supply and storage to reactor sales and advanced research.

- With such an agreement in place, Russia and the United States can plan and then implement long-term arrangements for spent-fuel storage, which would be a critical component of secure fuel-supply arrangements that can persuade countries to forgo their own enrichment and reprocessing facilities.

- Such an agreement would also enable the United States to approve the transfer to Russia of U.S.-origin spent fuel now held by friends such as South Korea and Taiwan.

- The United States should also work with Russia to assure that any fuel imported for storage is safe and secure, and that the revenue generated is used in part to sustain high levels of security for Russia's nuclear stockpiles over the long term.

Over the past fifteen years, the United States and Russia have created a foundation of practical cooperation to reduce nuclear risks of various kinds. The United States should try to expand this cooperation in the near future. Few Americans are aware that nearly half of the fuel for nuclear power plants that provide their electricity comes from dismantled Russian nuclear weapons.

Under the very successful Highly Enriched Uranium (HEU) Purchase Agreement—the "Megatons to Megawatts" Program—Russia is "blending down" a store of 500 tons of weapons-grade material so that it cannot be used for weapons but can be used to generate electricity. This agreement continues through 2013, but the United States should begin now to negotiate a new agreement that would accelerate the "blending-down" of the original 500 tons of weapons-grade material and extend the agreement to cover additional Russian HEU.

Finally, the United States must seek to engage Russia at the earliest possible date to reach an agreement on modernizing and enhancing programs to provide for the security of nuclear weapons, materials, and technology. The Cooperative Threat Reduction (CTR) programs conceived in the early 1990s by Senators Sam Nunn and Dick Lugar are outstanding examples of successful U.S.-Russian security cooperation and can offer major benefits to both sides for years to come. But they cannot and should not survive forever in their present form. The donor-client relationship of the 1990s is not a viable model for the future.

Sustained cooperation in this area will require that Washington and Moscow reach agreement on a new legal framework, on common standards of security, on transparency, on increased commitment of resources, and on broadening the reach of existing programs.

- The CTR umbrella agreement, under which several critical bilateral programs are conducted, is expiring in June 2006. The two sides should agree to extend this for a significant period—long enough to conduct a searching joint review of present and future program needs. Flexibility will be needed on both sides so that tough issues (such as liability protections for Americans working on CTR projects) do not block future cooperation.

- A modernized CTR effort will require a more even balance of resources from Russia and other donors. Russia's investment of its own resources has increased as its economy has improved. But Moscow will have to assume a greater share of the burden, even if other governments sustain resource commitments at existing levels.

- Building on their agreement at Bratislava in February 2005, the United States and Russia should agree on a common standard of security that each will provide and sustain for all nuclear weapons and weapons-usable materials on its territory, so that stockpiles are protected against threats that terrorists and criminals have shown they can pose.

- There are inevitable limits to the access that each government will grant the other to sensitive facilities, but disagreements over this issue must not be permitted to jeopardize improved security arrangements. Unless Russia overcomes its lack of transparency with respect to military facilities formerly associated with the Soviet biological weapons program, cooperation on bio-security will do little to make either country safer.

- Finally, U.S.-Russian cooperation should extend to third countries. The two sides are already working together to send Soviet-origin

HEU fuels back to Russia from research reactors in other countries and to convert such reactors to operate on fuel that cannot be used in nuclear weapons. Securing potentially vulnerable nuclear materials and installations anywhere in the world should be a U.S.-Russian priority.

Nuclear Weapons Dialogue

Nuclear materials and nuclear reactors already play a larger role in U.S.-Russian relations than do nuclear weapons themselves, and this is all to the good. Strategic force levels are at their lowest since 1991, and the Moscow Treaty of 2002 calls for still deeper cuts. The Bush administration's desire to keep arms control negotiations from becoming a divisive bilateral issue is a sound one.

All the same, the fact that both Russia and the United States are primarily worried about weapons of mass destruction in the hands of others is no reason to stop thinking about existing arsenals in each country. A revived high-level nuclear dialogue is necessary to address issues concerning the size, structure, and transparency of the two sides' nuclear forces.

Tactical nuclear weapons are the place to start. Fifteen years after the parallel commitments of Presidents George H.W. Bush and Mikhail Gorbachev, the United States has a clearer idea of the dimensions and disposition of the (probably) thousands of battlefield nuclear weapons in Russia's arsenal—but not clear enough. These weapons are a potential source of leakage into the hands of terrorists or proliferators and, despite renewed Russian doctrinal interest in using these weapons to compensate for deficiencies in conventional forces, their large numbers contribute very little to either side's security.

- A renewed nuclear dialogue may produce a formal new agreement, an elaboration of earlier parallel statements, or merely an improved understanding of each side's thinking and practices. Whatever its result, the dialogue should aim to serve the objectives of the Bush-Gorbachev declarations, the Nunn–Lugar programs, and the Moscow

Treaty: transparency, secure storage, and force reductions as instruments for scaling back each side's reliance on nuclear weapons in national defense.

- A high-level nuclear dialogue should address other issues as well. These include resuscitation and implementation of the 2000 agreement on exchanging ballistic-missile launch data, an assessment of the impact on stability of existing early-warning capabilities, and the need to anticipate the expiration both of the Strategic Arms Reduction Treaty I (START I) in 2009 and of the Moscow Treaty in 2012.

Counterterrorism Cooperation

Some of the terrorist groups that target Russia and the United States have a similar agenda, ideological origins, and modus operandi. They sometimes work together; so should those who are their targets. This conviction—that Russia and America face a common threat—was the basis of expanded cooperation after September 11. It still holds true today.

Although a group like ours cannot—and in fact should not be able to—provide an informed assessment of U.S.-Russian cooperation in this area, military and intelligence professionals on both sides recognize the significant common interest that requires them to cooperate. Yet three recent developments together represent a warning about the way in which the two sides are cooperating.

The first is the seeming Russian effort to curtail U.S. and NATO military access to Central Asian bases.

- Central Asian governments originally offered such access in 2001 as a way of assisting the military campaign against the Taliban. These same governments are now apparently under pressure to stop doing so.

- It is hard to understand the Russian desire to deny access at this stage except as a retreat from the idea that success in Afghanistan serves a common interest.

- American policy should seek a public Russian reaffirmation that this common effort has to continue for as long as necessary to achieve success and that Central Asian governments are right to be part of it.

A second warning of a possible divergence on the issue of counterterrorism is President Putin's invitation of the leaders of Hamas to Moscow.

- Were U.S.-Russian policy coordination high, this difference in diplomatic approaches might have been less significant.
- But with Russia having already shown that it will subordinate joint counterterrorism efforts to other goals, the invitation to Hamas is part of a worrying pattern.

A final warning is contained in the now-widespread Russian acknowledgment that the security and stability of the North Caucasus region are more at risk than they were six years ago, when the second Chechen war began.

- Recurrent terrorist attacks in this region make clear how dangerous the situation is, and how ineffective Russian policy has been.
- The United States lacks sufficient knowledge of this problem to know how best to address it, but one thing should be obvious to all—nothing threatens the future of Russia more than a strategy that spreads the military disaster that has engulfed Chechnya to the entire North Caucasus (even if the situation inside Chechnya is somewhat stabilized in the process). Yet that is what current Russian policy seems to be achieving.

Addressing the issue of Chechnya with President Putin has unfortunately been a dead-end for many years. It needs to be an early priority for high-level discussion with his successor.

Russia's Periphery: NATO, China, and Post-Soviet Neighbors

In eastern Europe, the Caucasus, Central Asia, and East Asia, the United States may find itself increasingly at odds with Russia in the coming half-decade. Across Russia's entire periphery, U.S.-Russian disagreement has recently become more the norm than the exception, and this negative trend is likely to continue. Such rivalry serves few American interests and should be avoided where possible, since it strengthens the influence and outlook of those within the Russian elite who dislike cooperation with the United States in the first place.

Yet American preferences may not matter much. Russian policy has shown such a high degree of competitiveness in these regions that increased friction between Moscow and Washington may prove inevitable. In this context, the real challenge for U.S. policy will be to advance American interests even in the face of friction, not to eliminate the friction altogether.

The United States should not cede a veto or undue deference to Russia over American relations with the states of the Russian periphery. Russia's legitimate interests deserve respect, but there is nothing legitimate about limiting the opportunity of its neighbors to deepen their integration into the international economy, to choose security allies and partners, or to pursue democratic political transformation.

- The United States should seek to accelerate the integration of countries into transatlantic and all-European institutions, if their foreign policies and domestic achievements demonstrate their readiness to contribute to these institutions.

- The contributions of states such as Ukraine, Georgia, Azerbaijan, Kazakhstan, and Moldova—to Balkan peacekeeping, to military campaigns in Afghanistan and Iraq—have already demonstrated that they can be valuable partners of the United States.

Increased frictions on Russia's periphery should also have implications for the future of cooperation between NATO and Russia. Joint participation in exercises and other operational and technical contacts between military personnel continue to have value, but the standing granted to Russia in a political forum such as the NATO-Russia Council needs to be more carefully scrutinized.

- The council's agenda should certainly not include issues that affect the interests of other post-Soviet states—least of all those aspiring to become members of the alliance—without their participation.

- Because 2007 will mark the fifth full year since the creation of the NATO-Russia Council, it is an appropriate moment for members of the alliance to review the council's record and to evaluate its achievements. This review needs to hold the council to a high standard. If its performance has been poor because Russia's approach is too different from those of other members—lacking in commitment to democratic principles or to the goal of collective responses to meet common challenges—NATO should seek other ways of consulting and cooperating with Russia.

The single most important country on Russia's periphery is, of course, China. The future policies and direction of these two countries will determine whether the group of the world's leading powers is divided into two sub-blocs based on their political systems—the democratic states and the authoritarian ones—or even into two military groupings. This prospect is still remote, but there are elements of the relationship between Russia and China that, if extended indefinitely, would begin to harden such distinctions.

- For instance, while the United States and Europe consult closely to coordinate their policies on the transfer of military equipment to China, Russia has found China to be an irresistible market for high-tech weapons exports.
- While the United States and Europe have sought, with considerable success, to speak with one voice to Central Asian states on issues of human rights, religious freedom, and the rule of law—especially within the framework of the Organization for Security and Cooperation in Europe (OSCE), to which all these states belong—Russian and Chinese policies treat these efforts as examples of "destabilizing" outside interference.

Preventing the division of the major powers into two camps is an authentic American interest, and efforts to advance it will succeed only if they reflect the interests of Russia and China as well. American strategy toward each country must therefore be based on the goal of making each one's relations with the United States at least as vital and productive as their relations with each other.

Pursuing stronger relations on the basis of common interests need not, however, prevent the United States from making clear when its interests diverge or from recognizing when theirs do. It is hard to imagine that it will indefinitely be American policy to reduce obstacles to high-tech cooperation with Russia (for example, on NATO-theater missile defense) if its military cooperation with China deepens. And while China probably shares Russian perspectives on Central Asian politics, it may not have quite as intense a geopolitical obsession with curtailing NATO access to military bases in the region.

Over the long term, the biggest single deterrent to the emergence of two camps among the major powers is most likely Russian awareness that such an outcome would make Russia more vulnerable and less able to protect its economic and security interests. It should be American policy to make clear to Russian leaders the advantages of being part of a single "club" of major powers—and the risks of dividing it.

Recommendations 2: Energy, Trade, and Environmental Cooperation

Energy Security

Russia is the world's largest exporter of natural gas and second-largest exporter of oil, and it should therefore play a central and positive role in global energy markets. To this end, the United States should seek to reinvigorate the U.S.-Russian strategic energy dialogue, giving it high-level attention and an ambitious agenda that brings benefits to both sides.

- The goal of this revived dialogue should be to strengthen the energy security of the United States, which depends on strong global production, diverse sources of supply, effective markets, fair and consistent treatment of foreign investors, cooperation on crisis management, the physical security of energy infrastructure, and more efficient use of resources by itself and other industrialized economies.

- A meaningful dialogue has to address Russian policies and practices that may be making the goal of energy security harder to realize. These include slowing growth rates in the energy sector, transportation bottlenecks, wasteful energy use, and the many difficulties that foreign companies face doing business in Russia.

Recent developments in the Russian energy sector—the state's increased dominance of the oil and gas sector as well as the confrontation with Ukraine—make it essential that the United States and its allies tackle a further element of energy security as well: preventing the politically motivated manipulation of supplies. Russia's actions make it unwise to rely on verbal assurances—even at a high level—that it will not exploit its energy resources for political purposes. Transparency and corporate governance in the Russian energy sector, which were once issues of concern mainly for investors and law-enforcement agencies, have become questions of national security as well.

Russia is seeking to expand its dominant position in the European natural gas market and to become a significant exporter of liquefied natural gas to the United States. While the United States should welcome increased Russian supplies to the world market, it must support—and encourage—Europe in its effort to diversify supplies and reduce the risk that Russia will use energy as a tool of state power. The United States should also join the European Union's call for Russia to ratify the European Energy Charter Treaty, which it signed more than a decade ago.

Because Russian energy companies, under increasing state control, cannot be treated as purely commercial entities, they demand especially strict scrutiny by the financial regulatory agencies of Western governments. More and more of these companies are seeking access to Western capital markets. They want to be listed on major exchanges and are initiating large public stock offerings. This process is positive, but only if exacting standards of disclosure and transparency are met. The U.S. and European governments should therefore work to harmonize disclosure requirements for listing companies on exchanges and for stock offerings. Unless it is associated with higher standards of corporate governance and commitment to commercial norms, increased access by state-controlled Russian companies to international capital will not serve Western interests. It will mean that international investors are financing the expansion of Russian state power and control.

Because of the negative impact of corruption in the Russian energy sector, the United States also should work with its G7 partners to gain Russian implementation of the standards of the Extractive Industries

Transparency Initiative (EITI), which was most recently endorsed by all members of the G8 at their 2005 Gleneagles summit.

- EITI is administered by a secretariat within the UK Department for International Development, with the cooperation of the International Monetary Fund (IMF) and the World Bank. It has been accepted by the other two principal energy exporters among former Soviet states, Azerbaijan and Kazakhstan; it has the further support of large and influential Western companies that are heavily involved in the Russian energy sector, including BP, Chevron, and ExxonMobil.

- No single initiative or mechanism of this kind can check official corruption, particularly as long as Russia's leaders do not themselves make it a priority. But given the corrosive impact of this issue on Russian development—and on its international integration—it should be American policy to upgrade attention to it. Initiatives that the Russian government has nominally endorsed offer a place to start.

The current slowdown in the growth of Russian oil and gas output runs the risk of becoming a long-term trend. To avert this, the U.S.-Russian energy dialogue should focus on factors that can facilitate investment—whether domestic or foreign—in exploration, development, and production.

- These include, among others, securing property rights and protections against disguised appropriation by the state, the stability of the legal and regulatory framework, taxation policy, licensing policy (including the revocation of licenses already granted), and the impact on management and innovation of increased state ownership.

- American policymakers need to emphasize the continuing negative impact of the Russian government's dismantlement of Yukos, which produced the largest market losses for minority shareholders of any act of nationalization in history. The damage done by the Yukos affair cannot be undone, but it should be a U.S. goal to get the Russian government to take serious and appropriate steps reflecting the harmful impact of its actions to date and repudiating arbitrary expropriations in the future.

A revived energy dialogue should also focus on other bottlenecks that limit Russian energy exports, including the capacity and control of its pipeline system.

- The United States should support Europe's call to open the gas transportation system to competition. The fact that energy transportation remains a state monopoly means that solutions depend on the ponderous and politicized decision-making processes of the Russian bureaucracy.

- OECD studies have linked this monopoly to the weak growth record of the Russian gas sector, which it calls the "least reformed" of the Russian economy. Without access to distribution and export networks, non-Gazprom producers have no incentive to invest.

More efficient energy use across the economy also has to have a place on the agenda of a U.S.-Russian dialogue.

- All industrial societies are examining the issue of energy efficiency, but Russia remains among the most wasteful users and furthest behind in adopting highly efficient technologies.

- The benefits for Russia of achieving modern levels of efficient energy use—and the benefits for our own and European security—would be enormous; if Russia used natural gas as efficiently as Canada, it would save three times the total amount of gas it exports to the European Union.

U.S. policy also needs to take better account of the difficulty that private industry has in resolving problem issues in energy cooperation with Russia.

- Energy cooperation continues to offer enormous potential benefits for both countries. Russian companies seek greater downstream opportunities in the West; American companies seek greater upstream opportunities in Russia.

- Yet the past several years have left Western business officials angry and frustrated at their experiences dealing with the Russian energy bureaucracy. Because they seek future favorable decisions from

Russian officials—and in fact from President Putin himself—they are often deterred from raising difficult issues. Less effective Russian policy—and lesser gains for both sides—are the predictable result.

- Given the strategic importance of energy security, American policymakers cannot treat obstacles to more effective U.S.-Russian cooperation as mere business issues.

WTO and Trade Liberalization

The United States should continue to promote Russia's accession to the WTO. Accession will promote further liberalization of the Russian economy and should signify full Russian acceptance of a rules-based international trading system. Such results will obviously benefit the United States; they may over time also help to strengthen political relations between the two countries.

American negotiators should not, however, attempt to resolve important remaining issues under the pressure of an artificial deadline, least of all the deadline of this year's G8 summit in St. Petersburg.

- Accession's positive results will be undermined if it is bestowed as a political reward or as a confidence-building measure offered in the hope of winning better performance in the future.

- It would be far better for the G8 meeting to come and go without Russia in the WTO, than to bring Russia into the organization on preferential terms.

Reaching an agreement based on strict economic and legal criteria is also important because once Russia joins the WTO, the administration will face the task of persuading Congress to support its "graduation" from the terms of the Jackson-Vanik amendment.

- This legislation was a successful and worthy element of American policy during the Cold War, and members of Congress will be understandably uncomfortable to cast a vote that signals acceptance of—or indifference to—Russia's retreat from democracy.

- We favor graduation, but believe that the administration will not be able to argue for it effectively unless it can demonstrate that the terms it negotiated bear no hint of a political reward, that it takes the deterioration of democracy in Russia seriously, and that it will respond effectively in other ways to this deterioration.

- If the administration fails to pay sufficient attention to Russia's authoritarian drift, it will leave American business with the worst possible result: Russia will be in the WTO, Jackson-Vanik will remain on the books, and the United States will for this reason be unable to make use of WTO mechanisms for resolving commercial disputes. American companies should not suffer in this way because U.S. policy has not taken due account of Russia's authoritarian drift.

WTO accession, though an important milestone, need not be the end of the process of trade liberalization with Russia. Once Russian accession is complete, the United States should propose to open a high-level joint review of the possible advantages of follow-on negotiations toward a bilateral Free Trade Agreement.

- Such an agreement could offer a strong further impetus for increased commerce as well as for greater competitiveness in both economies and for continuing liberalization within Russia.

- Special interests in both countries will raise objections to further openness, and because of such opposition the market impact of an agreement needs to be fully appreciated. But these adjustment costs should not block consideration of ways to deepen U.S.-Russian economic integration—a process that can bring important transformational benefits for both sides.

- The same sort of review should also be undertaken in parallel with governments of eastern Europe, Central Asia, and the Caucasus. The opportunity to reach agreement on accelerated liberalization may in fact be greater with these governments than with Russia.

Environmental Cooperation

Russia is the only member of the G8 without an independent environmental regulatory body. Abolishing the Committee on Environmental Protection was one of President Putin's first actions in this arena, and the decline in enforcement has had particularly serious consequences, coinciding as it does with strong economic growth and a surge in energy production. Over time Russia's poorly protected environment—including 20 percent of the world's fresh water, 20 percent of its forests, and the world's largest system of designated wilderness areas—will come under increased pressure because of the proximity of China, whose demand for energy, timber, and other resources is growing rapidly.

- The United States and other members of the G8 should make the case to Russian officials that reconstituting their own institutional capacity is an essential first step toward an effective strategy of environmental protection and resource management.

- It would also serve American interests to revive and reinvigorate the semi-moribund U.S.-Russian environmental agreement, negotiated by President Richard Nixon in 1972 and renegotiated by President Bill Clinton in 1994. Other important areas of cooperation should include stepped-up efforts in the management of jointly shared marine resources, such as those in the north Pacific and Bering Sea region.

- The joint committee that administers this bilateral environmental agreement should put energy issues at the top of its agenda—beginning with the development of a protocol to define and measure the environmental footprint of the oil and gas industry, promoting best practices in resource development, and identifying opportunities to develop alternative, sustainable energy projects in Russia.

- Special attention is needed to jointly address the issue of corruption in natural resources, which leads to illegal harvesting and trade in timber, fisheries, and other resources, including migratory fish and wildlife, some of which are part of shared U.S.-Russia populations.

Russia's Biological Diversity and Natural Resources

In terms of its environmental resources, Russia is a land of tremendous contrasts, having some of the world's best wilderness areas and a long history of nature protection while also containing some of the world's most polluted regions (Norilsk, Chelyabinsk, and others).

Nature Protection

Russia has the world's largest system of strictly protected areas, known as *zapovedniks*. Today these areas, along with other federally protected parks and preserves, cover more than 137 million acres and encompass 2.7 percent of the country's territory. No other country has devoted so much land to a network of highly restricted wilderness and a system of ecological research and monitoring. Many of the species recognized as endangered benefit from the protection of Russia's *zapovednik* system. Russia's vast and unpopulated areas play a globally important role for wildlife and biodiversity conservation. For example, three of the world's nine major migratory bird routes traverse Russia. Additionally, Russia contains some of the world's largest concentrations of natural resources, described below.

Forests

- Over 764 million hectares of forested lands (22 percent of the world's forest resources).
- Largest land-based carbon storage in the world (15 percent of the estimated global terrestrial capacity and 75 percent of total boreal forest capacity).
- Forest sector is of major global significance (21 percent of the world's standing timber volume; until recently, more than 10 percent of its total timber production).
- Russia's forests contain the most important habitats for Eurasia's bio-diversity.

Although Russia holds such a large share of the world's forests, according to the Russian Ministry of Natural Resources, only about 50 percent of the wood harvested in the country is processed domestically. This may account for the fact that Russia has only a 3 percent market share in the world's forest products market, in which it ranks ninth (after Canada, the United States, Germany, Finland, Sweden, France, Indonesia, and Austria).

The leading threats to Russia's forests are unsustainable forest practices such as illegal logging, human-caused fires, and industrial pollution.
- Up to 25 percent of the total volume of timber harvested in Russia is harvested illegally.
- Almost 2 million hectares of forest, mostly virgin, are logged in Russia annually.
- Over 5 million hectares are polluted with industrial and radioactive wastes.

Russia's Biological Diversity and Natural Resources (cont.)

Fresh Water
- Russia is second in the world after Brazil in the volume of its river resources. The country has about three million rivers and streams, and an average annual river-stream flow of 4,200 km^3.
- Russia has 26,500 km^3 of freshwater that is concentrated in 2.7 million lakes. The most prominent of Russia's freshwater bodies is Lake Baikal, the world's deepest and most capacious freshwater lake. Lake Baikal alone holds 85 percent of the freshwater resources contained in Russia's lakes and 20 percent of the world's total.
- Pollution of some rivers is still a major concern. For example, the Volga River's pollution level is still significant in the European part of Russia, despite lower production levels of local plants and factories in the post-Soviet period. The recent catastrophic pollution of the Amur River from sources in China showed that this problem has no borders.
- Poaching of freshwater fish species is also high. For example over 3,000 kg of poached sturgeon was recently seized in the Russian Far East.

Marine/Fisheries
- Russia is home to some of the most productive marine ecosystems in the world, including the Sea of Okhotsk, which has an extraordinary level of fish diversity, and the Bering Sea, which supports many transboundary marine wildlife species as well as significant economic resources for both the United States and Russia, including commercial fish species such as pollock and salmon.
- Fisheries comprise a critical component of the Russian Far East's economy. Key species harvested are pollock, herring, Pacific cod, bottom-dwelling fish such as halibut and flounder/sole, salmon, crab, and shrimp.
- In recent years, many of these fisheries have been subjected to severe overfishing, illegal fishing, unsustainable practices, and mismanagement. For example:
  - Continued use of large-scale driftnets for salmon fishing in both the domestic and Japanese fishing fleet is highly damaging to marine wildlife. Experts estimate that total mortality of seabirds in the Japanese fleet alone in the period from the late 1980s until 1997 exceeded one million birds. The Russian domestic drift-net salmon fleet is currently expanding.
  - Illegal trade in the fisheries industry, particularly in the Russian Far East, is on the rise. More than nine million rubles' worth of fish was confiscated from illegal trade in 2004. The growth of illegal trade of caviar is of particular concern to police, as revenues from illegal caviar sales are comparable to revenues from drug trafficking. In September 2005, the Ministry of Internal Affairs reported that 75 percent of seafood exported from the Russian Far East is illegal. Among these exports, 30 metric tons of illegal crab alone—worth $3 million—are sold monthly to Korea and Japan.

Russia's Biological Diversity and Natural Resources (cont.)

Mineral Resources

- Russia holds the world's largest natural gas reserves, with 1,680 trillion cubic feet (Tcf), nearly twice the reserves of the country with the next largest supply, Iran. In 2004, Russia was the world's largest natural gas producer (22.4 Tcf/y), as well as its largest exporter (7.1 Tcf/y).
- With 173 billion short tons, Russia holds the world's second-largest reserve of recoverable coal, behind only the United States, which holds roughly 274 billion short tons.
- Russia has the world's eighth-largest oil reserves and is the world's second-largest oil exporter. According to the *Oil and Gas Journal,* Russia has proven oil reserves of 60 billion barrels, most of which are located in western Siberia, between the Ural Mountains and the Central Siberian Plateau. Approximately 14 billion barrels exist on Sakhalin Island in the far eastern region of the country, just north of Japan.
- Russia also has extensive deposits of strategic minerals including gold, silver, platinum, cobalt, zinc, and mercury.
- Development of Russia's oil and gas sector is underway in several regions of particular importance for the environment. For example, numerous terminals are being constructed on the coast of the Barents Sea, one of the most productive northern marine ecosystems and among the world's richest fisheries. A pipeline from Lake Baikal to the Russian Far East is planned to traverse habitat for the rare Siberian tiger and endangered Amur leopard. On Sakhalin Island, construction of an onshore gas pipeline threatens spawning habitat for a rare salmonid fish, and offshore, a drilling platform has been constructed in the summer feeding grounds of the endangered Western Pacific gray whale, of which only one hundred individuals remain.
- Near the Caspian Sea, Chechnya has become a hot spot for environmental problems related to oil and the black market. Theft of oil from pipelines and refineries in Grozny is common. An estimated 30 million barrels of oil have leaked into the ground and unregulated "mini-refineries" contribute additional pollution, reportedly dumping refining wastes and contaminating the soil, water supply, rivers, and fish.

Russia's Biological Diversity and Natural Resources (cont.)

Agricultural Resources

Russia occupies more than one-tenth of the agricultural land on earth, including very large areas of rich and fertile soil. These regions have relatively favorable climatic conditions and high production and efficiency potentials. Cropping is improving, but the country's livestock products and processing industry cannot yet support world-market-quality goods, and to a great extent, Russia remains a net importer of food products.

Sources: World Bank, *Russia: Forest Policy during Transition*, World Bank Country Study, 1997; World Wildlife Fund (WWF), *The Russian-Danish Trade in Wood Products and Illegal Logging in Russia*, World Wildlife Fund Russia, 2003; World Wildlife Fund Russia, *Annual Report 2003*; http://www.svanhovd.no/abstracts/ab_2003/gov_2003/mnrnews_mar03.pdf; BBC Monitoring International Reports, January 25, 2006; Itar-Tass/SEAFOOD.com, October 15, 2004; http://www.eia.doe.gov/emeu/cabs/russia.html; various issues of *Russian Conservation News*; http://www.eia.doe.gov/emeu/cabs/russenv.html; and http://www.gfa-group.de/gfa_web_standardbeitrag/web_beitrag_2191.html.

Recommendations 3: Dealing with an Authoritarian Russia

Democratic Legitimacy

The Bush administration has been right to acknowledge, as it has done in the past year, Russia's retreat from democratic norms. As Russia enters a critically important political season—with parliamentary elections to be held next year and presidential elections in 2008—Western governments will have to give these questions still greater prominence, both publicly and privately.

Starting now, the United States should begin to work with its European allies to communicate publicly the main criteria that they will use for judging the legitimacy of this process. It will be hard to treat leaders who emerge from this process as fully legitimate if

- Opposition candidates are kept off the ballot on arbitrary or spurious grounds or removed from the ballot on the eve of the voting;
- Technicalities are used to deny registration to opposition political parties;
- Parties are blocked from forming electoral coalitions against the "party of power";
- Potential donors to opposition campaigns are threatened with retribution;
- Broadcast news coverage and advertising access are severely circumscribed; and

- Nonpartisan domestic monitoring organizations are kept from verifying electoral results.

All these practices represent the norm of Russian politics today, and they confront Russia, the United States, and Europe with the very real risk that Russia's leadership after 2008 will be seen, externally and internally, as illegitimate.

- The goal of Western governments must therefore be to win public commitments and specific, concrete actions by Russian officials to conduct the coming electoral cycle on an open, constitutional, and pluralist basis and to reverse the practices described above.
- Early and explicit discussion (comparable to the attention that was given, long before November 2004, to the integrity of Ukraine's political process) is far preferable to harsh but meaningless critiques on election day and the morning after.

The United States and other governments should make sure that their "democracy-promotion" assistance includes strong support for election-monitoring organizations—both inside and outside Russia. Legitimate elections depend on access by domestic monitors to all aspects of the electoral process.

- To be able to build an effective monitoring capability—especially the capacity to conduct parallel vote tabulation and professional exit polls—organizations such as Golos and the Levada Center need increased funds and technical assistance now.
- The European Network of Election Monitoring Organizations (ENEMO)—a coalition of seventeen observer groups from eastern Europe and post-Soviet states—should also be able to play a credible role in 2008.
- The United States should put its weight behind strengthening the OSCE. Although Russian officials have denounced it for its success in exposing electoral fraud in post-Soviet states, a robust OSCE is more needed than ever.
- The Russian government should be urged to give its full support to the "Declaration of Principles for International Election Observation and Code of Conduct for International Election Observers,"

a document endorsed by the UN secretary-general on October 27, 2005.

Western governments should not ignore the fact that efforts to portray the activities of election-monitoring organizations as "interference"—or even espionage—have had some success with Russian public opinion.

- To limit such perceptions, assistance should as much as possible not be disbursed directly by governments themselves, but by organizations with strong reputations for independence and impartiality.

- At the same time, the United States and its allies must stand their ground against official complaints and criticism and shift the rhetorical burden back on to those who try to limit openness and transparency.

President Bush has sought to bring "moral clarity" to the issue of democracy, but the impact of a single speech or press conference can be easily dissipated.

- Sustaining it requires continuing public attention to internal developments—and private communications that reinforce it as a priority. President Putin should not be able to say that no Western leader has expressed concern to him about the inconsistency between Russia's domestic evolution and the goals and principles of the G8.

- President Bush and other Western leaders should also diversify their political contacts within Russia. It is not enough to meet with representatives of "civil society." Open and routine contact with opposition political figures and organizations carry a more potent message to the Russian public and Russian elite.

Keeping alive the issue of democratic legitimacy in U.S.-Russian relations is not costly, but resources make the effort more effective.

- It is surprising to us, in light of the importance attached to promoting democracy, that the administration proposes to cut the Freedom Support Act yet again.

- The budget proposed for 2007 is barely one-third of what was spent in 2002.

Contact between Societies and Nongovernmental Organizations

Relatively free, unfettered, and expanding contact between NGOs in both Russia and the United States has been one of the most positive transformations in U.S.-Russian relations in the past fifteen years, and it has benefited both societies.

- The same kind of contact has characterized Russian relations with most European societies as well.

- Absent official interference, it will keep transforming—and normalizing—U.S.-Russian relations in the future, from the bottom up.

But these benefits are not secure, and protecting them will take increased effort and high-level attention in the future.

- Although presidents and other officials routinely call for greater contact and mutual understanding between societies, Russian law and practice have become increasingly restrictive.

- President Putin's advisers call NGOs with foreign contacts a "fifth column" within Russian society, and while loud international protests in late 2005 led the Kremlin to soften legislation regulating NGOs, Russian organizations of all kinds remain highly vulnerable—at risk of being closed on the basis of bureaucratic rulings that they have a "political" purpose.

- With the onset of elections next year, harassment and closure of NGOs on such grounds is likely to increase.

President Putin's response to foreign criticism of the NGO bill carries a double message.

- Russians officials are sensitive to their international standing and are prepared to make policy adjustments to protect it.

- At the same time, the reasons that led them to want to curtail NGO activity in the first place have not gone away, and the concessions they made to foreign opinion will not keep them from returning to this issue.

American policymakers—in unison with their European counterparts—will also have to be prepared to return to it, and to make clear that a reversal of fifteen years of openness between societies would put Russia far outside the transatlantic mainstream.

Health, Educational Exchange, and the Future of American Assistance

The past five years have brought a basic—and basically positive—transformation in U.S.-Russian relations; the idea that Russia needs large infusions of assistance to meet a range of major public needs is simply out of date.

- The tasks of post-Soviet reconstruction are not much less than they used to be, but—with a few exceptions—American public resources are no longer available on a large scale to help Russia address them.

- Because of sustained economic growth, Russian resources—at least in principle—are.

With narrower horizons, the challenge for future American assistance is to make good use of much-reduced governmental resources, focus on areas where there is a significant transnational payoff, and try to leverage public-private efforts with small amounts of aid.

There is near-unanimity among practitioners that, of all forms of bilateral assistance, exchanges pay the highest return in the long run.

- We share this view and advocate the highest possible level of funding. But we also recognize the importance of exchanges in other regions, and even among other post-Soviet states.

- It may be difficult to expand government funding for exchanges, but cutting funds and the number of exchangees is a mistake. Because tight budgets require clear priorities, we have no trouble choosing among alternative programs: student exchanges deserve the highest priority.

Health and infectious diseases are another area deserving continued support, but even here—where needs are great—balance is necessary.

- More than 60 percent of U.S. Agency for International Development (USAID) health-care funding (and very large private donations) is already devoted to HIV/AIDS; the marginal assistance dollar should be spent on other problems.

As in many other areas, exchanges may offer the highest payoff, especially in helping public-health professionals deal with the severity of Russia's demographic decline.

Finally, we call attention to the decline in the advanced training—in both Russia and the United States—of experts on the politics, history, and culture of the other.

- This is a reflection of the seeming normalcy of U.S.-Russian relations, and does not mean—as it would have during the Cold War—a decline in contacts or interest.

- But in the United States the U.S. policy establishment and American universities continue to need real expertise in Russian affairs. Russia's authoritarian direction makes this need particularly acute.

- Given these concerns, we strongly support the Secretary of State's recent addition of Russian to the list of languages deserving funding from the National Security Language Initiative budget.

Health and Demographic Trends in Russia

Population Decline. Russia's population has been plummeting for over a decade, by about 750,000 persons per year. This decline has been mitigated by significant immigration, making the excess of deaths over births even greater than that 750,000 figure. Long-term projections forecast a population decline to as little as 100 million by 2050, from the present population of 143 million. Demographic projections are notoriously unreliable, but there is reasonable certainty about the predictions for the near term (the next ten to fifteen years), since the women who will be of childbearing age in those years are little girls right now, and their numbers are declining.

One significant implication of declining raw numbers is conscription. Today, the Russian military drafts about 300,000 men per year. About two-thirds of all those eligible for the draft receive deferments of some kind. By 2015, there will be only a little over 600,000 eighteen-year-old males—so something has to change. (If two-thirds of those 600,000 defer, then there are only 200,000 left—leaving a 100,000-man deficit.) This creates a stark demographic impera-

Health and Demographic Trends in Russia (cont.)

tive for military reform. Either significantly fewer deferments must be granted, a hard political sell, or Russia must move away from conscription to the expensive and still-controversial proposition of more-professional armed forces.

Mortality Increase. The mortality increase of the last decade shows little sign of abating. The excess death rate is most significant among working-age men. For comparison: a sixteen-year-old boy in the United States has an 85–90 percent chance of reaching his sixtieth birthday. A sixteen-year-old boy in Russia has a 50 percent chance of turning sixty. Men are dying in what should be their prime productive years. The major causes of this excess mortality are cardiovascular disease and such "external causes" as industrial and workplace accidents, traffic accidents, suicide, homicide, poisonings, and other forms of trauma and injury.

A major underlying factor driving these causes of death is alcohol. The damage done by alcohol consumption cannot be understated, with patterns of drinking as much to blame as sheer quantity. A significantly disproportionate number of deaths take place on Sunday or Monday, after weekend binge drinking.

A Varied Picture. Russia's health and demographic patterns are far from homogeneous:

- *Geography.* Russia's regions vary greatly in their health and demographic statistics, and not always in predictable patterns. The Far East and Siberia, however, have suffered consistently and significantly lower life expectancies and higher population losses than European Russia.
- *Gender.* The life expectancy gap between men and women in Russia is the highest in the world. What bends women, breaks men. Alcohol is one major cause—men drink more and differently—though there are other factors. Researchers have yet to determine exactly why women have been more resilient.
- *Ethnicity.* Russia's Slavic population suffers lower life expectancy, lower birth rates, and higher mortality than its ethnic groups that are traditionally Muslim. Traditionally Islamic ethnic groups make up just over 10 percent of Russia's population, and that percentage is rising. Potential implications for politics and national security include the need to conscript more Muslims into the armed forces. The possibility of higher birth rates producing large cohorts of disenchanted, unemployed young Muslim men in the economically underdeveloped Muslim regions is another concern.
- *Socioeconomic status.* It is not as simple as wealth equals health. The rich and the small middle class are not uniformly healthier than the poor. But the rich do have access to decent health care, whereas the poor most definitely do not. The state health care system has crumbled.

Health and Demographic Trends in Russia (cont.)

HIV/AIDS. HIV/AIDS is a serious and growing issue, with over 1 percent of the adult population now infected. The fact that HIV is a compelling problem, however, does not doom Russia to the pandemic facing sub-Saharan Africa. Russia is quite different from Africa: Russians in general do not exhibit the same risky behaviors that many Africans do, and Russia has many advantages that Africa does not, including a literate population and extensive mass media for purposes of education and prevention campaigns, and a large, trained or trainable health workforce for delivering antiretroviral medications and other necessary care. This assumes, of course, that Russia will develop the political will to acknowledge and address its HIV problem—something that has yet to be demonstrated.

There is a danger that the HIV situation in Russia will receive disproportionate attention in comparison with more immediate health concerns, including chronic conditions, such as cardiovascular disease, that currently cause significantly higher rates of mortality. Most Russians, including the medical and public health community, do not rank HIV at the top of the list of health and demographic issues deserving the spotlight.

Not All Doom and Gloom. Some rays of hope have emerged in this gloomy picture, including a decline in infant/child/maternal mortality, some progress in dealing with tuberculosis, and a few regions that have made notable achievements in the delivery of health services. The key is committing the resources, political will, and most important, crucial infrastructural and systemic reform in the service of replicating these successes across the country's broad health and demographic landscape.

Conclusion

We have prepared this report to answer the difficult question of what policy should the United States pursue toward Russia.

Because we believe that Russia "matters," we have paid close attention to those problems that cannot be effectively addressed unless Moscow and Washington cooperate. Several of these are of critical importance—most notably, the threat posed by Iran's nuclear program and the risk that inadequately secured nuclear materials in Russia could fall into the wrong hands. The United States has every reason to preserve and expand such cooperation.

At the same time we have sought to identify those issues on which cooperation is becoming more difficult. There are many of these as well, and they shape our judgment that relations are headed in the wrong direction. In particular, Russia's relations with other post-Soviet states have become a source of significantly heightened U.S.-Russian friction. While avoiding unnecessary rivalry, American policy should counter Russian pressures that undermine the stability and independence of its neighbors and help ensure the success of those states that want to make the leap into the European mainstream.

In the next several years the most important negative factor in U.S.-Russian relations is likely to be Russia's emergent authoritarian political system. This trend will make it harder for the two sides to find common ground and harder to cooperate even when they do. It makes the future direction of Russian politics much less predictable.

If Russia remains on an authoritarian course, U.S.-Russian relations will almost certainly continue to fall short of their potential. Even today Russia's economic revival, political stability, and international self-confidence ought to have led to expanded cooperation on many fronts. Yet what has emerged instead is a relationship with a very narrow base. The large common interests that might animate a real partnership, including energy, counterterrorism, and nonproliferation, are frequently subordinated to other concerns of Russian policy—to internal struggles over property and power, to sensitivity about Russia's influence on its periphery, to anxieties about its looming political transition.

Drawing Russia into the Western political mainstream remains a critical interest of American foreign policy. Success would help the United States realize the promise of an undivided Europe, promote China's peaceful entry into the circle of great powers, and address a host of other major international problems. Only Russia can decide on a change of course, but other countries can help to frame its choice, making clear how much is to be gained—and how much has to be done. Doing so will be a long-term effort, but it should begin now, and the way to start is by talking about it. Russia's leaders—and its people—deserve to know what the world's real democracies think.

Additional and Dissenting Views

There is much to agree with in this thoughtful and comprehensive report, in particular the analysis and recommendations concerning security and energy, trade, and environmental cooperation. Where I part company with the consensus is the view that authoritarian trends in Russia have emerged as a central problem in the U.S.-Russian relationship. I do not disagree that Russia is a less democratic society than it was during the Yeltsin era. The question is what U.S. policymakers can actually do about it.

The answer, in my view, is very little. Indeed, making political reform a central issue in the U.S.-Russian dialogue is not only likely to be ineffective but may actually be counterproductive. In part, this is due to Russia's centuries-old political culture of centralization, secrecy, and paranoia. In recent years, these tendencies have been reinforced by the sense of humiliation and loss stemming from the end of the Cold War and the ensuing political and economic chaos in the country. Whether we like it or not, Vladimir Putin is perceived at home as having restored order and as using Russia's new strategic position as an energy supplier to rebuild the nation's international influence and prestige. Unfortunately, there is simply no strong constituency in Russia for pushing ahead with democratic reforms.

This is not to suggest that the vision of Russia as a more open and pluralistic society should be ruled out. As the report correctly notes, Russia's improved economic performance has led, for the first time in history, to a middle class that will inevitably press for the creation of a civic society that is necessary for genuine democratization. But this process will require one or two decades and can be driven only by liberalizing forces from within Russia itself.

Thus, at this stage of Russian development, U.S. policy should focus on areas of strategic convergence (terrorism, nonproliferation, and energy cooperation) and economic integration (the G8, the WTO, and trade and investment with the United States and the European Union) that will not only serve U.S. interests but bolster liberalizing forces in Russia. This, of course, does not mean that the move toward authoritarianism should not be on the U.S. agenda with Russia. The United States must always be able to defend and promote its core political values. But at this stage in the relationship, making democratization a central component of its policy toward Russia—as this report recommends—runs the risk of undermining our other critical objectives in working with Moscow.

Richard R. Burt

I endorse the general policy thrust of the report, which is, as I understand it, to continue and to expand U.S. engagement with Russia wherever it is possible to do so in a principled way, but not to shy away from clearly communicating to the Russians where the two countries have differences (such as in relation to Russia's recent record on democracy). I also believe that this is the general thrust of current U.S. policy toward Russia and that, while the report contains many constructive recommendations on how to advance that policy on both fronts, its claim to be suggesting a very different approach is somewhat overstated.

David R. Slade

The report seems—perhaps unintentionally—to assume that restricting Russian participation in multilateral meetings (notably the G8 but also the NATO-Russia Council) is a major source of leverage. No doubt Putin likes being in the G8, but we doubt that being excluded would have much impact on any action he cares much about. Similarly, if the

NATO-Russia Council, having served its purpose of helping Moscow acquiesce in NATO's inclusion of the Baltic states, has been unproductive of dialogue, much less cooperation, on security issues, NATO should let sleeping committees lie, dealing with issues affecting Russia's neighbors only in a NATO forum that includes those neighbors. Closing this or that "club" to Russia risks being an empty gesture—annoying Moscow without influencing it.

The report endorses facilitating U.S. private investment in Russian oil and other energy development as an aspect of "energy security." Of course, it is in the U.S. interest to increase total world oil production, but that is an exceedingly limited definition of "energy security," which also includes reducing world reliance on highly uncertain sources— the Middle East, but also Russia. It is unrealistic to think that the United States can promote an independent, oil-based industry center in Russia so powerful that it can defy the government (even assuming it would be either right or desirable to do so). Given all the other issues with Russia, making private oil investments less risky—while no doubt desirable in some very broad sense and certainly nice for the putative investors—is not a governmental priority on which it is worth expending much of the limited U.S. capacity to influence internal Russian arrangements.

In sum, it seems to us that the United States should accept that its main interests are not Russia's internal arrangements (though a more democratic and less corrupt Russia would probably serve U.S. interests, as it would certainly serve U.S. values). American foreign policy should cold-bloodedly realize that the United States and Russia have real differences and conflicts, but that that they can cooperate when they have de facto shared goals. The United States did that with the Soviet Union; it can as well with Putin's Russia. But it should do so without either illusions or paranoia.

Walter B. Slocombe
joined by
Robert D. Blackwill
Dov S. Zakheim

Task Force Members

Stephen E. Biegun is the Vice President for International Governmental Affairs at Ford Motor Company. He formerly served as National Security Adviser to Senate Majority Leader Bill Frist. He worked in the White House from 2001 to 2003 as Executive Secretary of the National Security Council and before that served for fourteen years as a foreign policy adviser to members of both the House of Representatives and the Senate. From 1992 to 1994, he was the Resident Director in the Russian Federation for the International Republican Institute.

Coit D. Blacker is Director of the Freeman Spogli Institute for International Studies and the Olivier Nomellini Family University Fellow in Undergraduate Education at Stanford University. He also serves as Cochair for Stanford's International Initiative. During the first Clinton administration, he served as Special Assistant to the President for National Security Affairs and Senior Director for Russian, Ukrainian, and Eurasian Affairs on the staff of the National Security Council.

Robert D. Blackwill* joined Barbour Griffith and Rogers International as President in November 2004, after serving as Deputy Assistant to the President and Deputy National Security Adviser for Strategic Planning under President George W. Bush. He also served as Presidential Envoy

Note: Task Force members participate in their individual and not their institutional capacities.
* The individual has endorsed the report and submitted an additional or a dissenting view.

77

to Iraq, as the Bush administration's coordinator for U.S. policies regarding Afghanistan and Iran, and as U.S. Ambassador to India. Prior to that, he was the Belfer Lecturer in International Security at Harvard University's John F. Kennedy School of Government.

Antonina W. Bouis is a consultant on cultural affairs involving Russia for businesses, museums, and nongovernmental organizations. She is coauthor of a new biography of Andrei Sakharov and translator of *Alexander II,* by Edvard Radzinsky. The founding Executive Director of the Soros Foundations (1987–92), she is Vice President of the Andrei Sakharov Foundation and a member of the advisory board of American Friends of the Tretyakov Gallery and the PEN Translation Committee.

Mark F. Brzezinski is a partner at the law firm of McGuireWoods LLP, where he manages the international law practice in Washington, DC. He served on the National Security Council staff in the Clinton administration, and from 1999 to 2000 served as its Director for Russia and Eurasia.

Richard R. Burt* serves as Chairman of Diligence, Inc., an international business intelligence and risk advisory services firm. He is also a Senior Adviser to the Center for Strategic and International Studies. He was U.S. Ambassador to the Federal Republic of Germany from 1985 to 1989 and, prior to this, he worked at the State Department as Assistant Secretary of State for European and Canadian Affairs. From 1977 to 1980, he worked in Washington as the national security correspondent for the *New York Times.*

John Edwards, Cochair of the Task Force, is the Director of the Center on Poverty, Work, and Opportunity at the University of North Carolina at Chapel Hill. He represented North Carolina in the Senate from 1999 to 2005. In 2004, he was chosen as the Democratic nominee for Vice President of the United States.

Robert J. Einhorn is Senior Adviser at the International Security Program of the Center for Strategic and International Studies. Previously, he served in the U.S. Department of State for twenty-nine years, and from 1999 to 2001, he was Assistant Secretary of State for Nonproliferation.

John Lewis Gaddis is the Robert A. Lovett Professor at Yale University, where he teaches Cold War history, grand strategy, and biography. His most recent book is *The Cold War: A New History*.

John A. Gordon served as the president's Homeland Security Adviser, as the Deputy National Security Adviser for Counterterrorism, and as the National Director for Counterterrorism. A retired U.S. Air Force General, he was Undersecretary of Energy and the first administrator of the National Nuclear Security Administration. He has also served as Deputy Director of Central Intelligence and spent thirty-two years in the Air Force with a concentration on research and development, strategic planning, missile and space operations, intergovernmental operations, and international negotiations.

James A. Harmon is Chairman of Harmon and Co., a financial advisory firm, and Chairman of the World Resources Institute, a global policy and research institution. He is also a Senior Adviser to the Rothschild Group, a global corporate advisory firm. He was Chairman and CEO of the U.S. Export-Import Bank from 1997 to 2001. From 1974 to 1986, he was a Partner of Wertheim and Co. (an investment bank) and was Chairman and CEO of Wertheim Schroder from 1986 to 1996. He is also a member of the boards of directors of a number of companies.

Steven E. Hellman is the Chairman and Cofounder of OILspace, a web-based technology solutions provider for the international oil industry (www.oilspace.com). He also cofounded one of the world's largest physical oil-trading companies, a real estate investment company operating in Russia and the United States, and a mortgage securitization company.

Fiona Hill is a Senior Fellow at the Brookings Institution in Washington, DC. She was previously Director of Strategic Planning at the Eurasia

Foundation. From 1991 to 1999, she held various positions at Harvard University, including Associate Director of the Strengthening Democratic Institutions Project at the John F. Kennedy School of Government, Director of Harvard's Project on Ethnic Conflict in the former Soviet Union, and Coordinator of Harvard's Trilateral Study on Japanese-Russian-U.S. Relations.

Jack Kemp, Cochair of the Task Force, is Founder and Chairman of Kemp Partners, a strategic consulting firm that seeks to provide clients with strategic counsel, relationship development, and marketing advice in helping them accomplish business and policy objectives. From January 1993 until July 2004, he was Codirector of Empower America, a Washington, DC–based public policy and advocacy organization he cofounded with William Bennett and Ambassador Jeane Kirkpatrick. Prior to that, he served as Secretary of Housing and Urban Development and represented New York in the House of Representatives for eighteen years. In 1996, he received the Republican Party's nomination for Vice President of the United States.

Clifford A. Kupchan is Director for Europe and Eurasia at the Eurasia Group, the political risk consultancy. Previously, he served as Vice President of the Nixon Center, and before that worked on Russian affairs at the U.S. Department of State.

Jessica T. Mathews is President of the Carnegie Endowment for International Peace, which in addition to its Washington, DC, headquarters, maintains a forty-person office in Russia: the Carnegie Moscow Center. Previously, she worked on Capitol Hill, in two presidential administrations, as a member of the Editorial Board and as a columnist for the *Washington Post*, and for ten years as Vice President and Director of Research at the World Resources Institute.

Michael A. McFaul is the Peter and Helen Bing Senior Fellow at the Hoover Institution, where he codirects the Iran Democracy Project. He is also the Director of the Center on Democracy, Development, and Rule of Law at the Freeman Spogli Institute and an Associate

Professor of Political Science at Stanford University. He is also a nonresident Senior Associate at the Carnegie Endowment for International Peace.

Mark C. Medish is a partner at the law firm Akin Gump Strauss Hauer and Feld LLP in Washington, DC, and a Visiting Scholar at the Carnegie Endowment for International Peace. He served on the staff of the National Security Council as Senior Director for Russian, Ukrainian, and Eurasian Affairs from 2000 to 2001, and worked at the Department of the Treasury as Deputy Assistant Secretary for International Affairs from 1997 to 2000. He also served as a Senior Adviser at the U.S. Agency for International Development and the United Nations Development Programme from 1994 to 1996. Prior to that, he practiced law at Covington and Burling.

Stephen Sestanovich, Director of the Task Force, is the George F. Kennan Senior Fellow for Russian and Eurasian Studies at the Council on Foreign Relations. He is also Kathryn and Shelby Cullom Davis Professor of International Diplomacy at Columbia University. From 1997 to 2001, he served as Ambassador-at-Large and Special Adviser to the Secretary of State for the Newly Independent States.

David R. Slade* is a Project Finance Partner in the New York office of Allen and Overy, an international law firm. He focuses on oil and gas and other natural-resource and energy-infrastructure projects in the states of the former Soviet Union, frequently acting for the U.S. Export-Import Bank and the Overseas Private Investment Corporation. He and his firm have worked on the Russian Oil and Gas Framework Agreement, the Vysotsk oil terminal, the Caspian oil pipeline, the Kovyka gas pipeline, the Sakhalin oil projects, and the Azeri early oil and BTC pipeline projects, among others.

Walter B. Slocombe* is a member of the Washington, DC, law firm of Caplin and Drysdale, Chartered. He has held a variety of senior positions in the Department of Defense, including Undersecretary of Defense for Policy from 1994 to 2001. During May–November 2003, he worked in Baghdad as the Coalition Provisional Authority's Senior Adviser for National Security and Defense. He has also served on the Presidential Commission on Intelligence Capabilities Regarding Weapons of Mass Destruction.

Strobe Talbott is President of the Brookings Institution. He served as Deputy Secretary of State from 1994 to 2001 and, before that, as Ambassador-at-Large and Special Adviser to the Secretary of State for the Newly Independent States. He has written several books on U.S.-Soviet relations, as well as *The Russia Hand: A Memoir of Presidential Diplomacy*.

Judyth L. Twigg is Associate Professor and Associate Director at the L. Douglas Wilder School of Government and Public Affairs at Virginia Commonwealth University. Her work focuses on issues of health, demographic change, and health care reform in Russia. She has been a consultant to the World Bank, the U.S. government, and several leading nongovernmental and research organizations.

Margaret D. Williams directs the World Wildlife Fund's Bering Sea Program and Russia projects. She serves as the Chair of the WWF's Arctic team and is also editor of *Russian Conservation News*, a quarterly journal. Previously, she served as a consultant to the World Bank on biodiversity projects in Central Asia and Macedonia.

Dov S. Zakheim* is Vice President of Booz Allen Hamilton, a global strategy and technology consulting firm. From 2001 to 2004, he served as the Undersecretary of Defense (Comptroller) and Chief Financial Officer for the Department of Defense. He previously served as Deputy Undersecretary of Defense for Planning and Resources (1985–87).

Task Force Observers

Derek H. Chollet
Center for Strategic & International Studies

James M. Goldgeier
Council on Foreign Relations

James R. "J.T." Taylor
Kemp Partners

Recent Independent Task Force Reports
Sponsored by the Council on Foreign Relations

More than Humanitarianism: A Strategic U.S. Approach Toward Africa (2006). Anthony Lake and Christine Todd Whitman, Chairs; Princeton N. Lyman and J. Stephen Morrison, Project Directors

In the Wake of War: Improving U.S. Post-Conflict Capabilities (2005). Samuel R. Berger and Brent Scowcroft, Chairs; William L. Nash, Project Director; Mona K. Sutphen, Deputy Director

In Support of Arab Democracy: Why and How (2005). Madeleine K. Albright and Vin Weber, Chairs; Steven A. Cook, Project Director

Building a North American Community (2005). John P. Manley, Pedro Aspe, and William F. Weld, Chairs; Thomas P. d'Aquino, Andrés Rozental, and Robert A. Pastor, Vice Chairs; Chappel A. Lawson, Project Director. Cosponsored with the Canadian Council of Chief Executives and the Consejo Mexicano de Asuntos Internacionales

Iran: Time for a New Approach (2004). Zbigniew Brzezinski and Robert M. Gates, Chairs; Suzanne Maloney, Project Director

Renewing the Atlantic Partnership (2004). Henry A. Kissinger and Lawrence H. Summers, Chairs; Charles A. Kupchan, Project Director

Nonlethal Weapons and Capabilities (2004). Graham T. Allison and Paul X. Kelley, Chairs; Richard L. Garwin, Project Director

New Priorities in South Asia: U.S. Policy Toward India, Pakistan, and Afghanistan (2003). Frank G. Wisner II, Nicholas Platt, and Marshall M. Bouton, Chairs; Dennis Kux and Mahnaz Ispahani, Project Directors. Cosponsored with the Asia Society

Finding America's Voice: A Strategy for Reinvigorating U.S. Public Diplomacy (2003). Peter G. Peterson, Chair; Jennifer Sieg, Project Director

Emergency Responders: Drastically Underfunded, Dangerously Unprepared (2003). Warren B. Rudman, Chair; Richard A. Clarke, Senior Adviser; Jamie F. Metzl, Project Director

Chinese Military Power (2003). Harold Brown, Chair; Joseph W. Prueher, Vice Chair; Adam Segal, Project Director

Iraq: The Day After (2003). Thomas R. Pickering and James R. Schlesinger, Chairs; Eric P. Schwartz, Project Director

Threats to Democracy (2002). Madeleine K. Albright and Bronislaw Geremek, Chairs; Morton H. Halperin, Project Director; Elizabeth Frawley Bagley, Associate Director

America—Still Unprepared, Still in Danger (2002). Gary Hart and Warren B. Rudman, Chairs; Stephen Flynn, Project Director

Terrorist Financing (2002). Maurice R. Greenberg, Chair; William F. Wechsler and Lee S. Wolosky, Project Directors

Enhancing U.S. Leadership at the United Nations (2002). David Dreier and Lee H. Hamilton, Chairs; Lee Feinstein and Adrian Karatnycky, Project Directors

Testing North Korea: The Next Stage in U.S. and ROK Policy (2001). Morton I. Abramowitz and James T. Laney, Chairs; Robert A. Manning, Project Director

The United States and Southeast Asia: A Policy for the New Administration (2001). J. Robert Kerrey, Chair; Robert A. Manning, Project Director

Strategic Energy Policy: Challenges for the 21st Century (2001). Edward L. Morse, Chair; Amy Myers Jaffe, Project Director

---

All publications listed are available on the Council on Foreign Relations website at www.cfr.org.
To order a bound copy, contact the Brookings Institution Press: 800-537-5487.